RESEARCH BIBLIOGRAPHIES & CHECKLISTS

14

Vicente Blasco Ibáñez: an annotated bibliography

RESEARCH BIBLIOGRAPHIES & CHECKLISTS

R&B

General editors

A.D. Deyermond, J.R. Little and J.E. Varey

July, 1977

*For my good friend Art,
whom I can never
thank enough for his
help on this bibliography.*

Paul

VICENTE BLASCO IBÁÑEZ

AN ANNOTATED BIBLIOGRAPHY

by

PAUL SMITH

Grant & Cutler Ltd
1976

© Grant & Cutler Ltd
1976

ISBN 0 7293 0015 3

I.S.B.N. 84-399-6349-1

DEPÓSITO LEGAL: V. 455 - 1977

Printed in Spain by Artes Gráficas Soler, S.A., Valencia

for

GRANT & CUTLER LTD
11, BUCKINGHAM STREET, LONDON, W.C.2.

Editors' Preface

* * *

The aim of this series is to provide research students and scholars with bibliographical information on aspects of Western European literature from the Middle Ages to the present day, in a convenient and accessible form. We hope to supplement, not to supplant, existing material. Single authors, periods or topics will be chosen for treatment wherever a gap needs to be filled and an authoritative scholar is prepared to fill it. Compilers will choose the form appropriate to each subject, ranging from the unannotated checklist to the selective critical bibliography; full descriptive bibliography is not, however, envisaged. Supplements will be issued, when appropriate, to keep the bibliographies up to date.

CONTENTS

Introduction   9

Primary Material
  Aa-Ac   Repudiated works   13
  Ac   Recognized works   19
  Ad   Correspondence   33
  Ae   English translations   35
  Af   Dramatizations and films 39
  Ag   BI's translations from French 41

Secondary Material
  Ba   Books, pamphlets, dissertations 43
  Bb   Articles, parts of books 63

Index of BI's works (Section B only)   125

Index of other writers   127

Introduction

In preparing this bibliography my purpose has been to provide an accurate and convenient guide for locating the works of Vicente Blasco Ibáñez and for identifying the significant critical writing about these works and their author. The period encompassed extends from 1882 through 1974. The bibliography is divided into the two sections outlined below:

A: Primary Material
  a Poetry
  b Drama
  c Prose (novels, stories, travel literature, history, speeches, etc.)
  d Correspondence
  e English translations for most of the prose fiction written after 1894
  f Dramatizations and films of Blasco Ibáñez's novels
  g Translations from French into Spanish by Blasco Ibáñez

B: Secondary Material
  a Books, pamphlets, Ph.D. dissertations, M.A. theses about Blasco Ibáñez exclusively or, in a few cases, substantially (25 per cent or more)
  b Articles and less substantial parts of books; other significant references or mentions

Within the subsections of A and B outlined above, all items are numbered consecutively for easy reference. Any item, primary or secondary, that I did not personally examine is followed by an asterisk. In addition, the following points pertain to certain subsections:

Ac The juvenilia repudiated by Blasco Ibáñez are listed chronologically by date of first publication, except for the few items that were published years after they were written. These are listed by date of composition. Whenever any repudiated work was later reprinted, this fact is always indicated. All of Blasco Ibáñez's recognized works are listed chronologically by year of first publication. For those which first appeared serially, the original form of serial publication and the first book edition are both indicated. Editions of

Blasco Ibáñez's 'complete' and collected works appear at the end of this section. Journalistic writing, which probably totals some 1400 items, is not included in this bibliography. For details of Blasco Ibáñez's journalism, see León Roca's *Blasco Ibáñez: política i periodisme,* Ba50.

Ba   Books, pamphlets, dissertations, and theses about Blasco Ibáñez or his works are listed alphabetically by author. When the author of a dissertation or thesis has also published a book, the book always appears first.

Bb   Articles are listed alphabetically by author. Anonymous articles are listed at the end of this section. Note that studies appearing in books are listed somewhat differently from those in periodicals:

(1)   Book item: Surname, forename, chapter title in single quotation marks, 'in', book title in italics, place of publication: publisher, year of publication, page numbers. E.g. Bb175 Eoff, Sherman H., 'VBI: *Cañas y barro* (1902)', in *The Modern Spanish Novel,* New York: New York Univ. Press, 1961, pp. 115-19.

(2)   Periodical item: Surname, forename, article title in single quotation marks, periodical title in italics, volume in Roman numerals, issue number in Arabic numerals, date in parentheses with English abbreviation (e.g. 2.5.58 = 2 May 1958), page numbers. E.g. Bb130 Chamberlin, Vernon A., 'Las imágenes animalistas y el color rojo en *La barraca*', *Duquesne Hispanic Review,* VI, 2 (Fall 1967), 23-36.

In this bibliography I employ, mostly in bibliographical entries, the following abbreviations:

B	Barcelona	BI	Blasco Ibáñez
BA	Buenos Aires	*EP*	*El Pueblo* (Valencian daily)
M	Madrid	*OC*	*Obras completas* (for BI's *OC*,
Val.	Valencia		ed. Aguilar, 3 vols)
Sp.	Spanish	VBI	Vicente Blasco Ibáñez

Of the few bibliographies hitherto available on BI, only one, by far the longest, requires mention here: that of J.L. León Roca, published as part of his biography, *VBI,* Ba51, pp. 620-60. The bibliography's major contribution is its listing of almost every item on BI that appeared (or even was mentioned) in the Republican daily *El Pueblo,* founded by the author in 1894. In fact, such items constitute a very major part of León Roca's bibliography. Here, however, I have attempted to discriminate between *El Pueblo* material of genuine biographical or literary significance and the majority of such pieces, which are often of ephemeral or local interest. I have excluded items in this latter category, especially within the extensive group of anonymous entries, from this bibliography. I have also eliminated many items which León Roca took from earlier bibliographies and lists but which in fact contain no reference, or at most a footnote, to Blasco Ibáñez: J.A. Balseiro's *Novelistas españoles modernos*; D. Daiches's *The Novel and the Modern World*; J.F. Montesinos's *Introducción a una historia de la novela en España en el siglo XIX*; H. Corbató's 'Some Outstanding and Recurring Themes in Valencian Literature', etc., etc.

In addition to articles from the Valencian press, I include items from news-papers in Madrid, Barcelona, and Saragossa, as well as from the press of Argentina (where BI lived for four years), Chile (native land of his second wife), the United States (where his translated works enjoyed spectacular success) and France (BI's spiritual homeland and his residence for some fifteen years). Moreover, all such secondary material is annotated except items I was unable to see. These are followed by an asterisk.

With two exceptions, this bibliography excludes references to BI in panoramic histories of Spanish literature. It includes, however, significant treatment or references to him in period histories of Spanish literature. Only important reviews of scholarly works about BI or his writings are included. Six Ph.D. dissertations, evidence of growing interest in BI, are scheduled for completion in 1975 or shortly thereafter. Peter Vickers's 'VBI: Literary Works and Ideology, 1880-1905', Univ. of London (Westfield College) promises to be an original, well documented and significant contribution to BI studies. Jean Vayssière's 'BI y Francia', Univ. of Dijon, will include new information about BI from French newspapers and journals. Fred Engel's 'The Republican Movement in Valencia, 1890-1912; the Origins of *Blasquismo* and the Development of Municipal Government in Spain', Univ. of California (San Diego) contains a number of shocking revelations about BI's political and personal activities in Valencia. Also in progress are Ralph Cherry's 'Characterization in BI's Valencian Novels', Carol Levert Langston's 'The Portrayal of Women in BI's Valencian Novels', both at Louisiana State Univ., and Linda B. Williams's 'Aspects of the Works of VBI', Univ. of Wisconsin (Madison).

Although this bibliography is intended to be selective rather than exhaustive, many items of genuine importance have doubtless escaped my attention. I hope, nevertheless, that this guide, with its 752 entries under secondary material alone, will represent an advance in breadth and accuracy over the unannotated biblio-graphies previously available. I hope too that it will prove useful to the increasing number of students who require a reasonably complete and accurate account of BI's own works, particularly his early repudiated writings.

I am indebted to Professor Rafael Ferreres for his many years of assistance and encouragement in my work on BI. To Don Rafael, a generous and exemplary Valencian, I dedicate with affection this bibliography on his *paisano*, VBI. Another person who helped me in a significant and selfless way, also over an extended period of time, is Professor Arthur L.-F. Askins of Berkeley. Professor Harvey Sharrer of Santa Barbara helped me locate a number of difficult items. Finally, Ricardo Carbonell Jordán and J.L. León Roca of Valencia, Peter Vickers, formerly of the University of Valencia (now at the British Council in Madrid), Professor Billy Thompson of New York, Fred Engel of La Jolla, and my colleagues in Los Angeles, Professors Rubén Angel Benítez and Robert Rudder, all provided valuable assistance. To each of them I express my sincere and deep appreciation.

A: PRIMARY MATERIAL

REPUDIATED WORKS

Unless otherwise indicated, BI repudiated all of his works published prior to 1895. Consequently, they do not appear in his *OC*. Reprints are indicated for the repudiated works where they exist. Most reprints of BI's early writings were issued by Ed. Cosmópolis shortly after BI died. Today they are rare.

a Poetry

Aa1   'A María', *La Ilustración Ibérica* (Jan. 87).
Sonnet to future wife.

Aa2   'Desde el destierro', *EP* (31.1.28).
Sonnet written in Paris during 1890-91 exile. First printed in *EP* after BI's death. Reprint: see Ba51, pp. 84-5.

Aa3   'En el centenario de Ribera', *El Correo de Valencia* (12.1.88).*

Aa4   'Serenata', *Almanaque de 'Las Provincias'*, Val., 1897.
Poem of 106 lines. Reprint: see Ba98, pp. 85-7.

b Drama

Ab1   *El juez*, Val.: Imprenta de Ripollés, 1894, 89 pp.

c Prose

Ac1   'La torre de la Boatella', *Lo Rat-Penat: Calendari llemosí corresponent al present any 1883*, Val., 1882, pp. 81-8.
Reprint in Valencian: see Ac129.

Ac2   'Fatimah', *Lo Rat-Penat: Calendari llemosí corresponent al present any 1884*, Val., 1883, pp. 106-25.
Reprint in Valencian: see Ac129; reprint in Sp. translation: see Ac17.

Ac3   'La rosa del certamen', *El Turia*, Val. (11.2.83).

13

Ac4   'Los talismanes (leyenda árabe)', *Almanaque de 'El Mercantil Valenciano'*, Val., 1884, pp. 257-63.

Ac5   *Carmen.* *

      E. Betoret-París, Ba9, pp. 33, 337, lists *Carmen* (1885) as BI's first published book. Neither Betoret nor others who mention this work (e.g. Just, León Roca, Tortosa) provide any specific bibliographical data on it. It is safe to presume that no copies of *Carmen* exist.

Ac6   'La misa de medianoche', *La Ilustración Ibérica* (Aug. 85).
      Reprint: see Ac17.

Ac7   'Un aria y un duo', *El Diablo Cojuelo*, Val., 2 (26.4.85), 11.

Ac8   'Un desencanto', *El Diablo Cojuelo*, Val., 1 (19.4.85), 10-11.

Ac9   'Aventura veneciana', *Almanaque de 'Las Provincias'*, Val., 1886.
      Reprint in *EP* (29.1.28).

Ac10   'Fray Ramiro', *La Ilustración Ibérica* (June 86).
      Reprint: see Ac17.

Ac11   'La noche de San Juan', *La Ilustración Ibérica* (Nov. 86).
      Reprint: see Ac17.

Ac12   'La nochebuena en Polonia', *La Ilustración Ibérica* (Dec. 86).

Ac13   'Las últimas notas', *La Ilustración Ibérica* (July 86).

Ac14   *El Conde Garci-Fernández, novela histórica del siglo X,* Val.: Imprenta de *El Correo de Valencia,* 1887, 404pp.
      Reprint: M: Cosmópolis, 1928, 294pp. Palau y Dulcet lists as 1st ed. that of 1888, which is actually a second ed. of 344pp.

Ac15   'Episodio maternal', *La Ilustración Ibérica* (Feb. 87).

Ac16   'La espada del templario', *Almanaque de 'Las Provincias'*, Val., 1887.
      Reprint: see Ac17.

Ac17   *Fantasías (leyendas y tradiciones),* Val.: Imprenta de *El Correo de Valencia,* 1887, 265pp.
      Reprint: M: Cosmópolis, 1928, 240pp. Under title *La misa de medianoche* Cosmópolis also published collection of four *leyendas* in its series 'El Libro de todos', 1928, 101pp. *Fantasías* contains eleven pieces, five of which (those preceded by 't') were previously published elsewhere, as indicated above:

           t 'La misa de medianoche'
             'Alvar Fáñez'

> t 'Fray Ramiro'
> 'Historia de una guzla'
> 'Tristán el sepulturero'
> 'La predicción'
> t 'Fátima' (previously in Valencian)
> 'El castillo de Peña Roja'
> t 'La espada del templario'
> t 'La noche de San Juan'
> 'In pace'

Ac18   'La muerte de Capeto', *La Ilustración Ibérica* (March-April 87).
Reprint: see Ac22.

Ac19   'El premio gordo', *La Ilustración Ibérica* (Dec. 87).

Ac20   'Un idilio nihilista', *La Ilustración Ibérica* (Sept.-Oct. 87).
Reprint: see Ac22.

Ac21   'El violinista', *La Ilustración Ibérica* (May-June 87).
Reprint: see note to Ac22.

Ac22   *El adiós de Schubert*, Val.: Imprenta de *El Correo de Valencia*,
1888, 436pp.
Reprint: M: Cosmópolis, 1928, 316pp. Contains novelettes 'El adiós
de Schubert' (whence title of collection) and 'Mademoiselle Norma'
plus shorter pieces: 'Un idilio nihilista', 'Marinoni', and 'La muerte de
Capeto'. Note that 'El adiós de Schubert' appeared first as 'El violinista'
in *La Ilustración Ibérica*, where 'Un idilio nihilista' and 'La muerte de
Capeto' also first appeared. Ed. Cosmópolis also reprinted the pieces in
the original *El adiós de Schubert* in various combinations, and some
even individually.

> 'El adiós de Schubert'
> 'Mademoiselle Norma'
> 'Un idilio nihilista'
> 'Marinoni'
> 'La muerte de Capeto'

Ac23   'El centenario de Ribera en Valencia', *La Ilustración Ibérica*
(Feb. 88).

Ac24   *Discurso de VBI: Danton MM*, Val.: Imprenta F.Vives, 1888,
17pp.

Ac25   *Hugo de Moncada*, Val.: Ediciones Lo Rat-Penat, 1933, 33pp.
Prize-winning biography read at 1888 'Jochs Florals'; remained unpublished until 1933.

Ac26   'Noche de invierno', *La Ilustración Ibérica* (Nov. 88).

Ac27   *¡Por la patria! (Roméu el guerrillero)*, Val.: Imprenta de
El Correo de Valencia, 1888, 387pp.
Reprint: M: Cosmópolis, 1928, 341pp.

Ac28   *Caerse del cielo, novela*, Val.: Imprenta de Luis Ortega, 1889,
264pp.
Forms part of the Biblioteca de *El Correo de Valencia*.

Ac29   'Amoríos en la luna', *La Ilustración Ibérica* (March 90).

Ac30   *Historia de la revolución española (desde la guerra de la
independencia a la restauración en Sagunto), 1804-1874* (con
un prólogo de D. Francisco Pi y Margall), 3 vols, B:Ed. La
Enciclopedia Democrática, 1890-2, 983; 935; 999pp.
Reprint in 13 vols; M: Cosmópolis, 1930-1. Notwithstanding title page,
Pi y Margall contributes an epilogue to vol. III rather than a prologue
to vol. I. Palau y Dulcet incorrectly dates first printing of vol. I as 1891.

Ac31   *Catecismo del buen republicano federal.* Val.: Imprenta de
Ripollés, 1892, 30pp.

Ac32   *La araña negra*, 2 vols, B:Ed. Seix, 1892-3, 1043; 1044pp.
Color plates by Eusebio Planas. Published first as 'cuadernos por entregas'
during indeterminate period. Reprint in 11 vols: M: Cosmópolis, 1928.
Reprint of *La araña negra* does not bear original title. Instead, each
volume has its own title as indicated below:

> *El conde de Baselga*
> *El padre Claudio*
> *El señor Avellaneda*
> *El capitán Alvarez* (2 vols)
> *La señora de Quirós*
> *Ricardito Baselga*
> *Marujita Quirós*
> *Juventud a la sombra de la vejez*
> *En París*
> *El casamiento de María*

Ac33   *París: Impresiones de un emigrado*, Val.: M. Senent, 1893,
285pp.
Only reprint: Mexico City: Prometeo, 1943, 286pp., with introduction
by Libertad Blasco Ibáñez. *París* . . . first appeared as a series of twenty-
four 'Crónicas de un emigrado' in *El Correo de Valencia* between 10.8.90
and 15.7.91.

Ac34   *¡Viva la República!*, 2 vols, Val.: M. Senent, 1893, 710;322pp.
Reprint in 4 vols: M: Cosmópolis, 1928. Each volume of reprint bears
a distinct title rather than that of original *¡Viva la República!* :

> *En el cráter del volcán*
> *La hermosa liejesa*
> *La explosión*
> *Guerra sin cuartel*

Ac35   *Los fanáticos*, 2 vols, B:Ed. Seix, 1895, 940; 936pp.
Color plates by Eusebio Planas. Published first as 'cuadernos por entregas'
during indeterminate period, probably 1893 and 1894, since it was
advertised as a continuation of *La araña negra*.

RECOGNIZED WORKS: INDIVIDUAL TITLES

No attempt is made to list here all authorized editions or reprints of BI's recognized works. Most of the recognized works were published by BI's own Ed. Prometeo and later in 3 vols of *OC* by Ed. Aguilar. The earlier works (1895-1909) were first published by BI's own Ed. Sempere, either in first editions or early reprints. Several of these works also appeared in BI's own 'La Novela Ilustrada' series. A small number of the early works were issued in reprints by other publishing houses, sometimes as part of a special collection. In Spanish America numerous unauthorized or pirate editions of BI's novels were issued.

Unfortunately, publishers sometimes made several editions of one of BI's works, either without giving the actual date of the impression or giving no date at all. For these reasons standard catalogs such as A. Palau y Dulcet's *Manual del librero hispanoamericano*, the *Catálogo general de la librería española*, and Mansell's *National Union Catalog of Pre-1956 Imprints*, vol. LX, are frequently unreliable as tools for accurately dating or distinguishing between different editions of BI's works.

This bibliography attempts to indicate the first book edition of each of BI's recognized works as well as any previous serial or periodical publication. It also lists major editions of his complete or selected works, but not editions primarily for student use. However, when such an edition has a noteworthy introduction or study, that fact is indicated under the editor's name in section Bb. BI's works are arranged in the following list alphabetically by year of first publication.

Ac36   *Arroz y tartana*, Val.: Biblioteca de *EP*, 1894, 442pp.
    First appeared in *folletín* of *EP* from 12.11.94 to 31.1.95, with book publication following shortly afterwards, although book bears date 1894.

Ac37   'Argel', *EP*, from 14.5.95 to 22.5.95.
    'Argel' is general title given seven Algerian sketches listed below. Reprint:

see note to Ac43 and also Ac128.

> Argel, el viaje
> En el puerto. El mercado. La kaasba
> La cueva de Cervantes
> La fiesta de Morabito
> Las mezquitas
> El mercado de Maison Carrel
> La kaasba de noche. Los guavos. Las dos Repúblicas

Ac38   'La caperuza', *EP* (4.3.95).
Reprint: see Ac43.

Ac39   'La corrección', *EP* (30.9.95).
Reprint: see Ac43.

Ac40   ' ¡Cosas de hombres!', *EP* (11.3.95).
Reprint: see Ac43.

Ac41   *Flor de Mayo*, Val.: Biblioteca de *EP*, 1895, 287pp.
First appeared in *folletín* of *EP* from 10.11.95 to 15.12.95.

Ac42   *A la sombra de la higuera*, B: Antonio López, editor, n.d. [1896?], 184pp.
Above title was given to a selection of seven of the nine original *Cuentos valencianos* (lacks only 'La cencerrada' and 'La apuesta del *esparrelló*'): see Ac43. *A la sombra de la higuera* appeared as no. 70 in the 'Colección Diamante' and was probably published about the same time as *Cuentos valencianos*.

Ac43   *Cuentos valencianos*, Val.: Imp. M. Alufre, 1896, 249pp.
Printings of the 1st ed. (Nov. 1896) contain, besides nine Valencian stories, seven pieces published earlier in *EP* under general title 'Argel': see Ac37. Here, however, they appear under the designation 'El país de Barbarroja'. These Algerian sketches are deleted from post-1902 eds of *Cuentos valencianos*, but were reprinted recently: see Ac128. The four Valencian stories below that are preceded by 't' appeared previously in *EP*. All post-1902 eds of *Cuentos valencianos* replace the deleted Algerian sketches with four stories, three of which were published elsewhere between 1899 and 1901. Regarding the fourth, 'En la puerta del cielo', translated from the original Valencian, see Ac129.

>   'Dimoni'
> t ' ¡Cosas de hombres!'
>   'La cencerrada'
> t 'La apuesta del *esparrelló*'
>   (original title:'La leyenda del *esparrelló*')

t 'La caperuza'
'Noche de bodas'
t 'La corrección'
'Guapeza valenciana'
'El *femater*'

First edition only:
  'El país de Barbarroja'
    Argel, el viaje
    En el puerto. El mercado. La kaasba
    La cueva de Cervantes
    La fiesta de Morabito
    Las mezquitas
    El mercado de Maison Carrel
    La kaasba de noche. Los guavos. Las dos Repúblicas

Post-1902 editions:
  'En la puerta del cielo'
  'El establo de Eva'
  'La tumba de Alí-Bellús'
  'El dragón del Patriarca'

Ac44 *En el país del arte (tres meses en Italia)*, Val.: no publisher stated, 1896, 288pp.
Most of the thirty-nine chapters were first published in the *folletín* of *EP* from 30.3.96 to 5.6.96.

Ac45 'La leyenda del *esparrelló*', *EP* (2.7.96).
Reprint: see Ac43.

Ac46 'La barca abandonada', *El Liberal* (8.8.97).
Reprint: see Aa63.

Ac47 'La condenada', *El Liberal* (6.6.97).
Reprint: see Aa63.

Ac48 'Desde Toledo', *EP*, from 23.5.97 to 29.5.97 and from 20.6.97 to 28.6.97.
Following pieces are not part of BI's *OC*. Reprint: see Ac128.

      La ciudad regia
      La Catedral
      La Catedral por dentro
      El Cardenal Albornoz y Don Alvaro de Luna
      Santa María la Blanca y San Vicente Ferrer
      Corpus toledano
      El mesón del Sevillano

El Alcázar
Las obreras de la muerte

Ac49 'El despertar del Buda', *EP* from 4.2.97 to 10.2.97.
Reprint: see Ac63.

Ac50 'En la boca del horno', *El Liberal* (12.9.97).
Reprint: see Ac63.

Ac51 'En el mar', *El Liberal* (25.7.97).
Reprint: see Ac63.

Ac52 'Golpe doble', *El Liberal* (3.5.97).
Reprint: see Ac63.

Ac53 ' ¡Mátala!', *El Imparcial* (May 97).
Not in any edition of BI's *OC.* Reprint: see Bb308.

Ac54 'El milagro de San Antonio', *El Liberal* (13.6.97).
Reprint: see Ac63.

Ac55 'El ogro', *El Liberal* (4.7.97).
Reprint: see Ac63.

Ac56 'El parásito del tren', *El Liberal* (11.7.97).
Reprint: see Ac63.

Ac57 'Primavera triste', *El Liberal* (30.5.97).
Reprint: see Ac67.

Ac58 'El pudridero de los reyes', *EP* from 20.4.97 to 23.4.97.
Under this title appear three pieces not included in any edition of BI's
OC. Reprint: see Ac128.

Camino del Escorial
El Faraón español
La gran pirámide española

Ac59 *La barraca*, Val.: Sempere, 1898, 300pp.
Published in *folletín* of *EP* from 6.11.98 to 24.11.98. Appears as book
on 17.11.98, one week before serial publication ends.

Ac60 'La paella del *roder*', *EP* (1.8.98).
Reprint: see Ac63.

Ac61 'Un funcionario', *El Liberal* (2.1.98).
Reprint: see Ac67.

Ac62 'Un silbido', *El Liberal* (6.2.98).
Reprint: see Ac63.

Ac63 *Cuentos grises*, Val.: Aguilar, n.d. (March 1899), 237pp.

Appears as vol. 91, Biblioteca Selecta. Of the thirteen stories in *Cuentos grises*, nine (those preceded by 't') appeared first (as indicated above) in the Madrid daily *El Liberal* between 3.5.97 and 6.2.98, not in *EP*, as León Roca states in the bibliography of his study; Ba51, p. 609. Most of these stories were also published in *EP* but it was at least several days after their appearance in *El Liberal*. 'La paella del *roder*' and 'El despertar del Buda' appeared first in *EP*. There were no reprints of *Cuentos grises* and most of its stories went to make up the collection, *La condenada*, 1900, Ac67, which was reprinted many times and constitutes part of BI's *OC*.

t 'Golpe doble'
t 'La barca abandonada'
   'La paella del *roder*'
   ' ¡Hombre al agua!'
t 'El parásito del tren'
t 'En el mar'
t 'Un silbido'
t 'El ogro'
t 'En la boca del horno'
t 'La condenada'
t 'El milagro de San Antonio'
   'El maniquí'
   'El despertar del Buda'

Ac64 'Lobos de mar', *Blanco y Negro*, 440 (7.10.99).
Reprint: see Ac67.

Ac65 'La pared', *Blanco y Negro*, 434 (26.8.99).
Reprint: see Ac67.

Ac66 'La tumba de Alí-Bellús', *Blanco y Negro*, 447 (25.11.99).
Reprint: see Ac43.

Ac67 *La condenada*, M: Fernando Fé, and Val.: Sempere, n.d. [1900], 293pp.

Modern title: *La condenada y otros cuentos*. Consists of twelve stories taken from *Cuentos grises*, 1899, Ac63, from which it deletes only 'El despertar del Buda'. To these it adds five stories listed below. Those preceded by 't' appeared first in *El Liberal*; those preceded by 'tt' appeared first in *Blanco y Negro*, as indicated above.

t 'Primavera triste'
t 'Un funcionario'
tt 'Lobos de mar'

t 'Venganza moruna'
tt 'La pared'

Ac68   *Entre naranjos*, Val.: Sempere, 1900, 416pp.

Ac69   'El establo de Eva', *Blanco y Negro*, 434 (11.8.1900).
Reprint: see Ac43.

Ac70   *La barraca*, Val.: Sempere, 1901, 283pp.
First illustrated ed. of this novel; illustrations by A. Fillol.

Ac71   'El dragón del patriarca', *Blanco y Negro*, 505 (5.1.01).
Reprint: see Ac43, note and under 'Post-1902 editions'.

Ac72   *Sónnica la cortesana*, Val.: Sempere, n.d. [1901], 409pp.

Ac73   *Cañas y barro*, Val.: Sempere, n.d. [1902], 312pp.
Publication begins first in *folletín* of *El Heraldo de Madrid* on 1.12.02, thus partially antedating publication of novel on 11.12.02. Publication in *El Heraldo* concludes 2.3.03.

Ac74   *La catedral*, Val.: Sempere, 1903, 356pp.

Ac75   *El intruso*, Val.: Sempere, 1904, 420pp.

Ac76   'Recuerdos de viaje', *EP* from 3.8.04 to 11.8.04.
These impressions of BI's Andalusian and North-African trip are not included in his *OC*. Reprint: see Ac128.

En la sierra
Gibraltar
La calle Real
Los hebreos
La sinagoga
Tánger la blanca
El moro en armas
Los golfos de Tánger

Ac77   *La bodega*, Val.: Sempere, 1905, 452pp.

Ac78   *La horda*, Val.: Sempere, 1905, 385pp.

Ac79   *La maja desnuda*, Val.: Sempere, 1906, 412pp.

Ac80   *Oriente*, Val.: Sempere, 1907, 355pp.
Despite imprint date, book was first placed on sale in Jan. 1908. The Madrid daily *El Liberal* previously published twenty of the book's thirty-three chapters, nineteen of them from 27.8.07 to 20.11.07, and one chapter on 1.1.08.

Ac81　'La rabia', *Los Lunes de 'El Imparcial'* (20.5.07).
Reprint: see Ac88.

Ac82　'El sapo', *Los Lunes de 'El Imparcial'* (27.5.07).
Reprint: see Ac88.

Ac83　*La voluntad de vivir*, Val.: Sempere, 1907. *
For personal reasons, BI ordered all copies of this novel destroyed shortly
before it was scheduled to appear. From probably the only preserved
copy, an edition with some name changes and other revisions was later
published: *La voluntad de vivir*, B: Planeta, 1953, 377pp. Not in *OC.*
See also Ac125.

Ac84　'Compasión', *Los Lunes de 'El Imparcial'* (10.2.08).
Reprint: see Ac88.

Ac85　*Sangre y arena*, Val.: Sempere, 1908, 410pp.

Ac86　*Conferencias completas dadas en Buenos Aires por el eminente
escritor español don VBI*, BA:A. Grau, 1925, 188pp.
Not in *OC.* Reprint: Ac127.

Ac87　*Las conferencias de VBI en el Paraguay*, Asunción: Grebour y
Schauman, 1909, 48pp. *
Not in *OC.*

Ac88　*Luna Benamor*, Val.: Sempere, 1909, 263pp.
The novelette *Luna Benamor* first appeared in *Caras y Caretas*, BA, 535
(2.1.09) unpaginated, with illustrations. Book editions of *Luna Benamor*
include six *Cuentos* and five *Bocetos y apuntes*. Those preceded by 't'
were first published in 1907 and 1908 in *Los Lunes de 'El Imparcial':*

> *Cuentos*
> t 'Un hallazgo'
> 'El último león'
> 'El lujo'
> t 'La rabia'
> t 'El sapo'
> t 'Compasión'
>
> *Bocetos y apuntes*
> 'El amor y la muerte'
> 'La vejez'
> 'La madre tierra'
> 'Rosas y ruiseñores'
> 'La casa del labrador'

Ac89　*Los muertos mandan*, Val.: Sempere, 1909, 430pp.

Ac90   *Argentina y sus grandezas*, M: Ed. Española-Americana, 1910, 768pp.

Large book with maps, plates, engravings, photographs, etc. Not in *OC.* Reprint in less expensive edition: B.A., Peuser, 1943, 201pp.

Ac91   *Los argonautas*, Val.: Prometeo, 1914, 597pp.

Ac92   *Historia de la Guerra Europea de 1914*, 9 vols, Val.: Prometeo, n.d. (also 1914-21).

Not in *OC*. This profusely illustrated work was first published serially as *cuadernos* at 50 céntimos each beginning 17.11.14. Some printings of book edition bear dates of 1914 or 1921.

Ac93   *Los cuatro jinetes del Apocalipsis*, Val.: Prometeo, 1916, 396pp.

The complete novel appeared in seventy installments in the *folletín* of *El Heraldo de Madrid* from 16.3.16 to 6.6.16. *Los cuatro jinetes* appeared as a book in April 1916, before serial publication concluded in *El Heraldo.*

Ac94   'El empleado del coche-cama', *La Esfera*, 130 (24.6.16).
Reprint: see Ac103.

Ac95   'El monstruo', *La Esfera*, 126 (27.5.16).
Reprint: see Ac103.

Ac96   'Noche servia', *La Esfera*, 128 (10.6.16).
Reprint: see Ac103.

Ac97   'El novelista', *La Esfera*, 139 (26.8.16).
No reprint.

Ac98   'Las vírgenes locas', *La Esfera*, 132 (8.7.16).
Reprint: see Ac103.

Ac99   *Mare Nostrum*, Val.: Prometeo, 1918, 446pp.

Although a printing of this same 446pp. ed. is reported in various bibliographies with a 1917 imprint date, *Mare Nostrum*, which BI finished writing in Dec. 1917, was not published until March 1918.

Ac100 *Los enemigos de la mujer*, Val.: Prometeo, 1919, 447pp.

Ac101 *Artículos sobre México*, ed. Enrique de Llano, Mexico City: Talleres Linotipográficos de *El Hogar*, 1920, 89pp.

Contains articles BI wrote during his visit to Mexico and published in *El Universal*. Not in *OC.*

Ac102 *El militarismo mejicano (estudios publicados en los principales diarios de los Estados Unidos)*, Val.: Prometeo, 1920, 250pp.

Ac103 *El préstamo de la difunta*, Val.: Prometeo, 1921, 291pp.
Contains fourteen pieces, four of which (preceded by 't') were first published in *La Esfera* in 1916:
>'El préstamo de la difunta'
>t 'El monstruo'
>'El rey de las praderas'
>t 'Noche servia'
>'Las plumas del caburé'
>t 'Las vírgenes locas'
>'La vieja del *cinema*'
>'El automóvil del general'
>'Un beso'
>'La loca de la casa'
>'La sublevación de Martínez'
>t 'El empleado del coche-cama'
>'Los cuatro hijos de Eva'
>'La cigarra y la hormiga'

Ac104 'La familia del doctor Pedraza', M: La Novela de Hoy, no.25, 1922, 79pp.
Reprint: see Ac109.

Ac105 *El paraíso de las mujeres*, Val.: Prometeo, 1922, 337pp.

Ac106 *La tierra de todos*, Val.: Prometeo, 1922, 356pp.

Ac107 'El comediante Fonseca', M: La Novela de Hoy, no.58, 1923, 61pp.
Reprint: see Ac109.

Ac108 *La reina Calafia*, Val.: Prometeo, 1923, 301pp.

Ac109 *Novelas de la Costa Azul*, Val.: Prometeo, 1924, 301pp.
Contains six pieces, two of which (preceded by 't') were first published in series of La Novela de Hoy:
>'Puesta de sol'
>t 'La familia del doctor Pedraza'
>'El sol de los muertos'
>t 'El comediante Fonseca'
>'El viejo del paseo de los Ingleses'
>'En la Costa Azul'

Ac110 *Una nación secuestrada (el terror militarista en España)*, Paris: J. Durá, impresor, 1924. *
Not in *OC.* Reprint: see Ac114.

Ac111 *La vuelta al mundo de un novelista*, 3 vols, Val.: Prometeo, 1924-5.

Ac112 *Lo que será la República Española (al país y al ejército)*, Paris: Casa de la Democracia, 1925, unpaginated (32pp).
This pamphlet was supposedly printed (and also put into circulation) clandestinely by a certain Ed. Gutenberg, Val. Not in *OC*. Reprint: see Ac114.

Ac113 *El Papa del Mar*, Val.: Prometeo, 1925, 327pp.

Ac114 *Por España y contra el rey*, Paris: Ed. Excelsior, 1925, 242pp.
Under the above title BI publishes together items previously published individually. Not in *OC*.

> *Una nación secuestrada.* See Ac110.
> *Lo que será la República Española.* See Ac112.
> *España con Honra*: seven articles from BI's
> revolutionary newspaper published in Paris:
>   'La pluma y la revolución'
>   'Ladridos junto al camino'
>   'La verdad en marcha'
>   'El rey contesta al novelista'
>   'Alfonso XIII intenta perseguirme en Francia'
>   'Contestación a M. Poincaré'
>   'A un amigo de Alfonso XIII'

Ac115 *A los pies de Venus*, Val.: Prometeo, 1926, 341pp.

Ac116 *Novelas de amor y de muerte*, Val.: Prometeo, 1927, 309pp.
Of the following six *novelas*, the first five were published one a month from Feb. to June 1926 in the illustrated booklet series of La Novela de Hoy. The sixth, 'El despertar del Buda', dates from 1897: see Ac49.

>   'El secreto de la baronesa'
>   'Piedra de Luna'
>   'El rey Lear, impresor'
>   'La devoradora'
>   'El réprobo'
>   'El despertar del Buda'

Ac117 *En busca del Gran Kan (Cristóbal Colón)*, Val.: Prometeo, 1929, 279pp.

Ac118 *El caballero de la Virgen (Alonso de Ojeda)*, Val.: Prometeo, 1929, 322pp.

Ac119 *El fantasma de las alas de oro*, Val.: Prometeo, 1930, 293pp.

Ac120 *Estudios literarios*, Val.: Prometeo, 1934, 396pp.

RECOGNIZED WORKS: COLLECTED WORKS, etc.

The following editions of BI's selected or complete works are arranged chronologically by date of edition.

Ac121 La Novela Ilustrada, Madrid, 1905-8.

One of BI's own publishing enterprises, La Novela Ilustrada, published and distributed by subscription very cheap editions of Spanish novels and Spanish translations of popular American and European authors. BI included at least the following five of his own novels in this series. Typically, they bear no imprint date:

> *Arroz y tartana*
> *La barraca*
> *Flor de Mayo*
> *La maja desnuda*
> *Sónnica la cortesana*

Ac122 *Obras completas*, 39 vols, Val.: Prometeo, 1923-34.

Prometeo published all of BI's works that had previously been published by Ed. Sempere and by its successor, Prometeo itself. The exception is *Historia de la Guerra Europea de 1914*, Ac92. For complete list of works in the Prometeo *OC*, see Ac124.

Ac123 Colección Austral, B.A.: Espasa-Calpe, 1943-4.

Espasa-Calpe of Argentina issued seven of BI's earlier novels. There have been many reprints but these novels have not been available in Spain.

> *Arroz y tartana*
> *La barraca*
> *Cañas y barro*
> *La condenada*
> *Cuentos valencianos*
> *Entre naranjos*
> *Sangre y arena*

Ac124 *Obras completas*, 3 vols, M: Aguilar, 1946.

These leather-bound, bible-paper editions of BI's 'complete' works

contain a large majority but not all of BI's recognized works. This
edition includes in vol. I a 'Nota biobibliográfica' which mostly reproduces BI's 1927 letter to I. López Lapuya: see Ad3. Each vol. has
been reprinted several times without any changes from the 1946 first
edition. Vol. I, which contains the most popular works, has had to date
at least seven printings. The works listed below were also published in
39 vols by Prometeo, Ac122. In that Prometeo edition of the *OC*, *Los
argonautas* was issued in two volumes and *La vuelta al mundo* in three
volumes.

Volume I

Cuentos valencianos
La condenada y otros cuentos
En el país del arte
Arroz y tartana
Flor de Mayo
La barraca
Entre naranjos
Sónnica la cortesana
Cañas y barro
La catedral
El intruso
La bodega
La horda
La maja desnuda

Volume II

Oriente
Sangre y arena
Los muertos mandan
Luna Benamor - Cuentos - Bocetos y apuntes
Los argonautas
Los cuatro jinetes del Apocalipsis
Mare Nostrum
Los enemigos de la mujer
El militarismo mejicano
El préstamo de la difunta y otros cuentos
El paraíso de las mujeres

Volume III

La tierra de todos
La Reina Calafia
Novelas de la Costa Azul
La vuelta al mundo de un novelista

> *Novelas de amor y de muerte*
> *El Papa del mar*
> *A los pies de Venus*
> *En busca del Gran Kan*
> *El caballero de la Virgen*
> *El fantasma de las alas de oro*
> *Estudios literarios*

Ac125 Colección de autores españoles contemporáneos, B: Ed.
Planeta, 1948-55.

During a seven-year period Ed. Planeta made available a large number
of BI's individual novels previously available in complete or collected
works editions only. Titles arranged in order of date of first edition:

> *Arroz y tartana*
> *En el país del arte*
> *La barraca*
> *Entre naranjos*
> *Sónnica la cortesana*
> *Cañas y barro*
> *La bodega*
> *La horda*
> * *La voluntad de vivir (novela póstuma)* See Ac83
> *Los argonautas*
> *La tierra de todos*
> *Los cuatro jinetes del Apocalipsis*
> *El préstamo de la difunta y otros cuentos*
> *El paraíso de las mujeres*
> *El Papa del mar*
> *A los pies de Venus*

Ac126 *Tres novelas valencianas*, M: Ed. Plenitud, 1958, 962pp.

> *Arroz y tartana*
> *La barraca*
> *Cañas y barro*

Ac127 *Discursos literarios*, Val.: Prometeo, 1966, 445pp.

This book, edited and with an introduction by E. Gascó Contell, reprints
BI's Argentine speeches (see Ac86) along with 'La novela y su influencia
social' and several subsequent speeches of little importance. Two appendices contain thirty brief commentaries on BI by his contemporaries
and a quite incomplete and inaccurate 'Tabla cronológica'.

Ac128 *Crónicas de viaje*, Val.: Prometeo, 1967, 282pp.

J.L. León Roca gathers together and reprints from BI's *EP* journalism four series of travel sketches, for which he provides the unifying title *Crónicas de viaje*. Regrettably, he fails to give any indication of their date of publication in *EP*. The dates and original heading (when different) of each section are supplied below:

'Gibraltar' (originally: 'Recuerdos de viaje') from 3.8.04 to 11.8.04. See also Ac76.

'Argel' from 14.5.95 to 22.5.95. See also Ac37.

'Toledo' (originally: 'Desde Toledo') from 23.5.97 to 29.5.97 and from 20.6.97 to 28.6.97. See also Ac48.

'El Escorial' (originally: 'El pudridero de los reyes') from 20.4.97 to 23.4.97. See also Ac58.

Ac129 *Narracions valencianes*, introduction by Alfons Cucó, Val: Impremta Fermar-Col·lecció Garbí, 1967, 100pp.

Cucó collects BI's only writings in Catalan. Of these four pieces, 'Lo darrer esforç' is reproduced from a manuscript copy and printed for the first time. 'En la porta del cel', which in Spanish translation forms part of BI's recognized works (see note to post-1902 eds of *Cuentos valencianos*, Ac43), was probably written between 1890 and 1894, but was not published in the original Valencian dialect until 1908, several years after its appearance in Spanish.

> 'La torre de la Boatella' See Ac1
> 'Fatimah' See Ac2
> 'Lo darrer esforç'
> 'En la porta del cel' See Ac43

CORRESPONDENCE

I Published Correspondence

Ad1   To Cejador y Frauca, Julio (6.3.18): in Bb128, pp. 471-8.
BI explains his ideas on the novel.

Ad2   To González, Joaquín V.: in *Boletín de la Academia Argentina de Letras,* VIII (1940), pp. 155-7. *
Letters on González's *Mis montañas* and other books.

Ad3   To López Lapuya, Isidro (1927): in BI's *OC*, I, pp. 9-12.
Confessional, autobiographical letter. First published by Pitollet as part of his article on BI: Bb423, pp. 237-41.

Ad4   To Llorente Olivares, Teodoro (?.9.95),(?.12.95), (31.1.07): in *Epistolari Llorente. Correspondència rebuda de 1861 a 1911 per En Teodor Llorente Olivares*, 2 vols, B: Biblioteca Balmes, 1928-9, pp. 252-3; 256; 124.
On the loss of BI's writing privileges when in jail; on *Flor de Mayo*; on anniversary of defense of Valencia against French invaders.

Ad5   To Maldonado de Guevara, Francisco (16.3.26): in Bb470, 75-6.
Acknowledges receipt of Maldonado's study on Columbus, which will be useful for finishing *En busca del Gran Kan*.

Ad6   To Martínez de la Riva, Ramón: in Ba56, pp. 159-81.
Seven letters from 1918 to 1927. BI in France discusses cinematography, his literary projects, and the life he leads.

Ad7   To Meliá Bernabeu, José [pseud: Pigmalión] (16.10.14), (?.11.14), (10.10.22), (30.8.23): in Ba59, pp. 119-20; 122-3; 128-31; 131-5.
About BI's *Historia de la Guerra Europea*; BI's interests as a collector; his plans for world tour.

Ad8   To Pérez Galdós, Benito: in Bb387, pp. 128-39.
Ten letters (some undated), nine written approximately 1902-7, one

in 1918. Letters deal with politics, literature, personal matters; 1918 letter on possible publication of *Tristana* by Ed. Prometeo.

Ad9 To Pitollet, Camille: in Ba73, pp. 59-129.

Collection of twenty-five letters translated into French by Pitollet. Some undated but most written between Jan. 1920 and May 1922. Letters stress how Pitollet was supposed to write BI's biography. Also touch upon Sp. authors, politics, etc. Several of these letters, complete or abbreviated, are reproduced (in the original Spanish) in the Sp. version of Pitollet's study on BI: see Ba75.

Ad10 To Precioso, Artemio: in Ba77, pp. 179-206.

Sixteen letters written from 1922 to 1927. Detailed information on editorial, publishing, financial, literary, political, and personal matters.

Ad11 To Valencia, the voters of (16.3.06): in Ba54, pp. 165-8.

Open letter of resignation as Republican deputy to Cortes.

Ad12 To Valdeiglesias, Marqués de (15.10.20): in Pilar Guirao Lozano's 'Archivo epistolar de Guillermo Fernández Shaw', *Revista de Literatura*, XXXIV, 67-8 (1958), 150.

Letter of recommendation for Rodríguez Beteta.

Ad13 To Zola, Emile (5.12.93): in Bb411, 53-4.

Letter in French seeking permission to publish Sp. translation of several of Zola's novels.

II Unpublished Correspondence

Ad14 To Alas, Leopoldo [pseud: Clarín] (2.16.95), (1900?), (1.17.01): in private archives of Don Gamallo Fierros, Madrid.

BI asks Alas for opinion on *Arroz y tartana*; thanks him for letter concerning *Entre naranjos*; thanks him for his praise in 'Palique' in *El Heraldo de Madrid*.

Ad15 To Unamuno, Miguel de (6.3.03), (?.2.03), (17.7.22), (26.8.22), (28.12.24): in Unamuno Archives, Salamanca.

First two letters on Rodrigo Soriano affair; others on proposed meetings between BI and Unamuno.

ENGLISH TRANSLATIONS OF BI's PROSE WORKS

Unless otherwise indicated, and notwithstanding an occasional title change, American and English editions of the same novel are the work of the same translator. Many of BI's stories were translated and published individually in American magazines and journals, but these, together with translations of excerpts or selections, are excluded from the following list, which includes integral editions only.

I Novels

Ae1   *A los pies de Venus*
       The Borgias: Or at the Feet of Venus. Tr. by Arthur Livingston. New York: Dutton, 1930. *At the Feet of Venus: A Tale of the Borgias.* London: Skeffington, 1931.

Ae2   *Arroz y tartana.*
       The Three Roses. Tr. by Stuart Edgar Grummon. New York: Dutton, 1932.

Ae3   *La barraca*
       The Cabin. Tr. by Francis Haffkine Snow and Beatrice M. Mekota. New York: Knopf, 1917. London: Hurst and Blackett, 1919.
       See also Bb531.

Ae4   *La bodega*
       La Bodega (The Fruit of the Vine). Tr. by Isaac Goldberg. New York: Dutton, 1919. London: Unwin, 1923.

Ae5   *El caballero de la Virgen*
       The Knight of the Virgin. Tr. by Arthur Livingston. New York: Dutton, 1930. London: Butterworth, 1931.

Ae6   *Cañas y barro*
       Reeds and Mud. Tr. by Isaac Goldberg. New York: Dutton, 1928. London: Butterworth, 1929.

Reeds and Mud. Tr. by Lester Beberfall. Boston: Humphries, 1966.

Ae7   *La catedral*
The Shadow of the Cathedral. Tr. by Mrs W.A. Gillespie. London: Constable, 1909. New York: Dutton, 1909. London: Unwin, 1923.

Ae8   *Los cuatro jinetes del Apocalipsis*
The Four Horsemen of the Apocalypse. Tr. by Charlotte Brewster Jordan. New York: Dutton, 1918, reprinted until 1962. London: Constable, 1919.

Ae9   *En busca del Gran Kan*
Unknown Lands: The Story of Columbus. Tr. by Arthur Livingston. New York: Dutton, 1929. London: Butterworth, 1931.
Novel first appeared in magazine *Cosmopolitan* from Nov. 1928 to March 1929. Both in the magazine and book publication the English version antedated the one in Spanish.

Ae10 *Los enemigos de la mujer*
The Enemies of Woman. Tr. by Irving Brown. New York: Dutton, 1920. London: Unwin, 1922.

Ae11 *Entre naranjos*
The Torrent. Tr. by Isaac Goldberg and Arthur Livingston. New York: Dutton, 1921. London: Unwin, 1923. New York: Burt, 1926.

Ae12 *El fantasma de las alas de oro*
The Phantom with Wings of Gold. Tr. by Arthur Livingston. New York: Dutton, 1931.

Ae13 *Flor de Mayo*
The Mayflower: A Tale of the Valencian Seashore. Tr. by Arthur Livingston. New York: Dutton, 1921. London: Unwin, 1922. New York: Burt, 1929.

Ae14 *La horda*
The Mob. Tr. by Mariano Joaquín Lorente. New York: Dutton, 1927. London: Butterworth, 1927.

Ae15 *El intruso*
The Intruder. Tr. by Mrs W.A. Gillespie. New York: Dutton, 1928. London: Butterworth, 1930.

Ae16 *La maja desnuda*
Woman Triumphant. Tr. by Hayward Keniston. New York: Dutton, 1920. London: Constable, 1921. New York: Burt, 1929.
The Naked Lady. Tr. by Frances Partridge. London: Elek, 1959.

Ae17 *Mare Nostrum*
Mare Nostrum (Our Sea). Tr. by Charlotte Brewster Jordan. New York: Dutton, 1919. London: Constable, 1920.

Ae18 *Los muertos mandan*
The Dead Command. Tr. by Frances Douglas. New York: Duffield, 1919. London: Unwin, 1923.

Ae19 *El Papa del mar*
The Pope of the Sea: an Historic Medley. Tr. by Arthur Livingston. New York: Dutton, 1927.

Ae20 *La reina Calafia*
Queen Calafia. Tr. anonymously. New York: Dutton, 1924. London: Butterworth, 1925.

Ae21 *Sangre y arena*
The Blood of the Arena. Tr. by Frances Douglas. Chicago: A.C. McClurg, 1911.
Blood and Sand. Tr. by Mrs W.A. Gillespie. London: Simpkin, Marshall, 1913.
Blood and Sand. Tr. by Frances Partridge. New York: Ungar, 1958. London: Elek, 1958. London: Mayflower Books, 1964.

Ae22 *Sónnica la cortesana*
Sónnica. Tr. by Frances Douglas. New York: Duffield, 1912. London: John Long, 1915.

Ae23 *La tierra de todos*
The Temptress. Tr. by Leo Ongley. New York: Dutton, 1923. London: Butterworth, 1933.

II Prose other than Novels

Ae24 *En el país del arte*
In the Land of Art. Tr. by Frances Douglas. New York: Dutton, 1923. London: Unwin, 1924.

Ae25 *Luna Benamor*
Luna Benamor. Tr. by Isaac Goldberg. Boston: J.W. Luce, 1919.

Ae26 *El militarismo mejicano*
Mexico in Revolution. Tr. by Arthur Livingston and José Padín. New York: Dutton, 1920.

Ae27 *El préstamo de la difunta*
The Old Woman of the Movies, and Other Stories. Tr. by José Padín, Arthur Livingston, Leo Ongley, and Harriet Wishnieff. New York: Dutton, 1926.

English title is taken from 'La vieja del *cinema*', whereas the Spanish version of this collection (Ac103) is named after another story. Five of the fourteen stories in the original collection are replaced by ones from other sources.

Ae28 *Una nación secuestrada: el terror militarista en España*
Alphonso XIII Unmasked!!! The Military Terror in Spain. Tr. by Leo Ongley. New York: Dutton, 1924. London: E. Nash and Grayson, 1925.

Ae29 *La vuelta al mundo de un novelista*
A Novelist's Tour of the World. Tr. by Leo Ongley and Arthur Livingston. New York: Dutton, 1926. London: Butterworth, 1927.

DRAMATIZATIONS AND FILMS OF BI's NOVELS

I Dramatizations

Af1 *La barraca.* Adaptation by José Jerique. *

Af2 *Cañas y barro.* Adaptation by V. Serrano Clavero. *

Af3 *La catedral.* Adaptation by Gonzalo Jover and V. Serrano Clavero. *

Af4 *Los cuatro jinetes del Apocalipsis.* B: Maucci, n.d., 128pp. Adaptation in five acts by Luis Linares Becerra.

Af5 *El endiablado; cuadro dramático basado en una novela de VBI.* Val.: M. Ferreró, 1901, 18pp. Adaptation by Ricardo Bayarri Pascual.

Af6 *Los enemigos de la mujer.* Adaptation by Eduardo Marquina. *

Af7 *La horda.* M: R. Velasco, 1913, 48pp. Adaptation in one act by Dionisio Laguía with music by Rafael Calleja.

Af8 *El intruso.* M: R. Velasco, 1906, 93pp. Adaptation in four acts by Gonzalo Jover and Emilio González del Castillo.

Af9 *Sangre y arena.* M: R. Velasco, 1911, 49pp. One-act *zarzuela*, divided into four *cuadros*. Adapted by Gonzalo Jover and Emilio González del Castillo.

Af10 *Sangre y arena según la novela de VBI.* B: Ed. Bistagne, n.d. [1949], 71pp. Author of dramatic adaptation not indicated.

Af11 *La tierra de todos.* B: Maucci, n.d. [1927?], 144pp. Adaptation in five acts by Luis Linares Becerra.

II Films

Af12 *La barraca* (1944). Mexico. Stars Anita Blanch, Domingo Soler.

Af13 *La bodega* (1930). France. Produced by Benito Perojo. Stars Conchita Piquer, Gabriel Gabrio.

Af14 *Blood and Sand* (1922). USA. Stars Rudolph Valentino,
Lila Lee.

Af15 *Blood and Sand* (1941). USA. Stars Tyrone Power,
Rita Hayworth, Linda Darnell.

Af16 *Cañas y barro* (1954). Spain. Stars Ana Amendola,
Virgilio Texiera.

Af17 *Enemies of Women* (1923). USA. Stars Lionel Barrymore,
Alma Roberts.

Af18 *Entre naranjos* (1914). Spain. Produced and directed by
Alberto Marro.

Af19 *The Four Horsemen of the Apocalypse* (1921). USA. Stars
Rudolph Valentino, Alice Terry, Wallace Beery.

Af20 *The Four Horsemen of the Apocalypse* (1962). USA. Stars
Glenn Ford, Ingrid Thulin, Charles Boyer.

Af21 *Mare Nostrum* (1926). USA. Stars Alice Terry, Antonio Moreno.

Af22 *Mare Nostrum* (1948). Italy-Spain. Stars Fernando Rey,
María Félix.

Af23 *Ni sangre ni arena* (1941). Mexico. Stars Mario Moreno,
'Cantinflas'. Spoof of film based on BI's novel?

Af24 *Sangre y arena* (1916). France. Adapted and produced by BI
in collaboration with Ricardo de Baños and José María
Maristany.

Af25 *The Temptress* (1927). USA. Stars Greta Garbo, Lionel Barrymore. BI's novel *La tierra de todos*.

Af26 *The Torrent* (1926). USA. Stars Greta Garbo, Antonio Moreno.
BI's novel *Entre naranjos*.

Ag1   Arouet, F.M. [pseud: Voltaire], *Diccionario filosófico*,
6 vols, Val.: Sempere — Imprenta de *El Pueblo*. 1901.

Ag2   Lavisse, Ernesto, and Alfredo Rambaud, *Novísima historia
universal*, 14 vols, Val.: Prometeo, 1908.

Loti, Pierre: see Viaud, Julien.

Ag3   Mardrus, J.C., *El libro de las mil y una noches*, 23 vols,
Val.: Prometeo, 1910.

BI's version, the first complete one in Spanish, was made from Mardrus's
1899 French translation from the Arabic.

Ag4   Michelet, J., *Historia de la revolución francesa*, 3 vols, Val.:
Biblioteca Popular, 1898.

Those bibliographies which list this work incorrectly give the 1900
Sempere ed. as the first Spanish translation.

Ag5   Reclus, Onésimo, and E. Reclus, *Novísima geografía universal*,
6 vols, M: Ed. Española-Americana — Imprenta de *La Novela
Ilustrada*, 1906-7.

Ag6   Viaud, Julien [pseud: Pierre Loti], *El ultraje de los bárbaros*,
Paris: Imprimerie de G. de Malherbe, n.d. (1917?), 31pp.

Voltaire: see Arouet, F.M.

Ag7   Wagner, Ricardo, *Novelas y pensamientos (músicos, filósofos
y poetas)*, Val.: Sempere, n.d. (1901?), 225pp.

BI made his translation from a French translation of the German.

B: SECONDARY MATERIAL

BOOKS, PAMPHLETS, Ph.D. DISSERTATIONS, etc., EXCLUSIVELY OR SUBSTANTIALLY ABOUT BI

Ba1 Akers, J.M., 'VBI as a Critic of Sp. Society and Institutions', Unpubl. M.A. thesis, Nottingham Univ., 1957. *

Ba2 Alcina Navarrete, José, *VBI: oración a su vida y a su muerte*, Alcoy: Imprenta Fraternidad, 1928, 40pp.
Homage to BI the politician; includes section on representative types of women in BI's novels.

Ba3 Archivo Municipal, Publicaciones de, *VBI*, Val.: Excm. Ayuntamiento, 1933, 62pp.
This booklet was issued to commemorate return of BI's remains for burial in Valencia. It contains a not always accurate 'Cronología de BI', selections from BI's works (some of which are translated into Valencian), and a number of opinions and commentaries favorable to BI.

Ba4 Baixauli, José, *BI en la intimidad*, Val.: Ed. Carceller, n.d., 31pp.
Contains several interesting anecdotes, but is very partisan in treatment of such topics as: BI, Don Carlos, and Pi y Margall; BI's hatred of Carlism; BI and money.

Ba5 Balseiro, José A., 'VBI', in *BI, Unamuno, Valle-Inclán, Baroja: cuatro individualistas de España*, Chapel Hill: Univ. of North Carolina Press, 1949, pp. 1-76.
Episodic, flamboyant treatment of BI's career and works. Makes some suggestive comparisons of certain of BI's novels to works by Zola and Galdós. See also Bb362.

Ba6 Bark, Ernesto, *BI*, 1896. *
Cited without further details by R. Pérez de la Dehesa in *El grupo 'Germinal': una clave del 98*, p. 37. Also listed on cover of Bark's pamphlet *Nicolás Salmerón*, M: Biblioteca Germinal, 1903, as a publication in the same series of 'Biografías Contemporáneas'.

Ba7 Beger, Iris, 'Der Regionalismus in Werke von VBI', thesis, Freie Univ. Berlin, 1957, 142pp. *

Ba8   Bernat, Luis, *Casiquisme roig*, Val.: Imprenta de *El Radical*, 1904, 169pp.
Discusses BI's manifesto 'La revolución de Valencia', corruption among BI's followers in municipal administration, how BI's party was running the city, etc.

Ba9   Betoret-París, Eduardo, *El costumbrismo regional en la obra de BI*, Val.: Fomento de Cultura, Ediciones, 1958, 344pp.
Mostly on BI's use of Valencian places, customs, festivals, traditions, language, etc., in his works. Although it says relatively little about BI's artistic elaboration of regional elements, this study is a thorough and important reference work, authenticating the circumstantial aspect of BI's writings. See also Ba10.

Ba10   ——, 'El costumbrismo regional de VBI', Unpubl. Ph.D. dissertation, Univ. of Kansas, 1957. *
No *DissA*. Revised form of this dissertation was published in 1958. See Ba9.

Ba11   ——, 'La tierra valenciana como escenario de las obras regionales de VBI', Unpubl. M.A. thesis, Univ. of Kansas, 1952. *

Ba12   Bopp, Eugene C., 'Traditional Lore and Customs of Spain in the Valencian Novels of VBI', Unpubl. M.A. thesis, Columbia Univ., 1933, 174pp. *

Ba13   Bruhn, William H., 'Structure as Style in Three Works of BI', Unpubl. Ph.D. dissertation, Univ. of Iowa, 1972, 235pp.
DissA, XXXIII,7 (1973), p. 3633A. Analyses BI's literary technique following methods of Percy Lubbock, Edwin Muir, and other modern critics. Treats one novel from each major period: *Flor de Mayo* (Valencian); *El intruso* (Spanish); *Los cuatro jinetes del Apocalipsis* (international). Asserts that the widely acclaimed artistic qualities of Valencian cycle are found in all of BI's writings. However, BI's political views and his works written for Hollywood cause his entire *oeuvre* to be underrated even today.

       Caballero Audaz, el [pseud.] : see Carretero, J.M.

Ba14   Cardwell, Richard A., *BI: La barraca*, Critical Guides to Spanish Texts, no. 7, London: Grant and Cutler in association with Tamesis Books Ltd, 1973, 95pp.
One of the most detailed and thorough studies of any of BI's novels. Provides an unusually complete and multi-faceted examination of *La barraca* in terms of its underlying socio-economic background and its

possible sociological and political interpretations. The connection of *La barraca* to naturalism is sensitively explored. Although literary aspects of *La barraca* are given less emphasis, the novel's structure, characters, and style are perceptively analysed. Major criticism on *La barraca* is well synthesized in this recommended study.

Ba15   Carretero, Enrique, *Paralelismo entre el escritor don VBI y un lacayo de la monarquía española apodado 'El Caballero Audaz'*, La Habana: Imprenta Alemana, 1925, 64pp. *

Ba16   Carretero, José María [pseud: El Caballero Audaz], *El novelista que vendió a su patria o Tartarín, revolucionario*, M: Ed. Renacimiento, 1924, 135pp.
Purportedly written to establish the truth about Spain, which BI supposedly besmirched in his *Una nación secuestrada*, this work portrays BI as an avaricious, cowardly, treacherous, gross, and traitorous man who accepted funds from Russian Communists to help spread revolution in Spain. See also Bb89.

Ba16a   Centre Nationale de Bibliographie, 'VBI', Les Bibliographies du Centre Nat. de Bibl., Brussels, no. 69.03 (1969), 5 mimeographed pp.
Lists most French translations of BI's works.

Ba17   Cola, Julio, *BI, fundador de pueblos*, M: Ed. Ambos Mundos, 1931, 134pp.
BI's secretary in Argentina tries to vindicate novelist's controversial colonizing efforts in Río Negro and Corrientes. Attributes BI's serious problems to Argentine political intrigues. Although it is biased, sometimes inaccurate, and lacks a clear chronological framework, Cola's apology remains the best source of information on BI's Argentine adventure outside Argentine newspapers of that period.

Ba18   Conde Gargollo, Enrique, *BI y el Madrid novecentista*, M: Imprenta 'El Arte', 1967, 27pp.
Evokes the political and literary scene in turn-of-the-century Madrid. Tells how BI's success affected his relationship with certain members of the Generation of 98. Contains little that is original.

Ba19   Cortina Gómez, Rodolfo, *BI y la novela evocativa, 'El Papa del mar' y 'A los pies de Venus'*, M: Ediciones Maisal, 1973, 149pp.
This is a revised version of author's Ph.D. dissertation with an added appendix on BI's prologues: see Ba20. Analyses use of two plots, 'una novelesca coetánea al autor y otra histórica' and how they are integrated.

By demonstrating novels' debt to cinematography rather than naturalism, Cortina shows BI's technique to be one of literary impressionism. Cortina's solid study also deserves attention as one of the few serious works along thematic, structural, and stylistic lines about BI's later novels.

Ba20 Cortina, Rodolfo José, 'BI: el primer momento de su serie de novelas evocativas', Ph.D. dissertation, Case Western Reserve Univ., 1971, 159pp.

DissA, XXXII,6 (1971), p. 3299A. This dissertation was published with revised title and added appendix: see Ba19.

Ba21 Curry, Virginia Frances, 'VBI: Social Reformer and Propagandist', Unpubl. Ph.D. dissertation, Indiana Univ., 1956, 193pp.

DissA, XVII,1 (1957), pp. 141-2. A social and humanitarian purpose informs not only the thesis novels but also BI's Valencian cycle and his trilogy on the World War. Catalogs the specific social and political institutions that BI attacks in each group of novels as part of his plan to reform Spain. Regrettably, the author of this dissertation lacks a clear sense of social history and this weakens her study.

Ba22 Dalbor, John Bronislaw, 'BI's Theory of the Novel and its Application in his Works', Unpubl. M.A. thesis, Pennsylvania State Univ., 1953, 182pp.

Treats major influences on BI's ideas about the novel, on his concept of the novelist, and on BI's own theories and practices. Gives reasons why BI was not an outstanding theorist and concludes that in general his theories and practices correspond.

Ba23 ——, 'The Short Stories of VBI', Unpubl. Ph.D. dissertation, Univ. of Michigan, 1961, 307pp.

DissA, XXII,7 (1962), pp. 2395-6. An excellent study on an overlooked aspect of BI's art. Provides, after a thorough introductory section on the short story in general, an internal literary analysis of BI's *cuentos* and an analysis of major themes, narrative technique, character presentation, etc. Dalbor finds that BI is not only better as a short-story writer than as a novelist, but that he is among the finest European short-story writers.

Ba24 Day, A. Grove, and Edgar C. Knowlton, Jr, *VBI*, Twayne World Authors Series, no. 235, New York: Twayne Publishers, 1972, 167pp.

This is the only over-all study of BI's life and works that is available in English. However, those familiar with BI's novels will find the excessive retelling of plot, lack of penetrating analysis, and the often imperfectly assimilated critical concepts of other scholars to be weaknesses of this study. See also Bb461.

Ba25 Domínguez Barberá, Martín, *El tradicionalismo de un republicano*, 3 vols, Sevilla: Ediciones Montejurra, 1961-2.
Domínguez, former editor of Valencia's daily *Las Provincias*, attempts a partial vindication of his fellow Valencian by trying to show that a vigorous Valencian and Spanish traditionalism underlies much of BI's 'tumultuous revolutionary Republicanism'. Each volume of this study has a different subtitle: I. *VBI*; II. *La tradición valentina*; III. *Valencia fuera de órbita*. Only vol. I and the second half of III deal primarily with BI. Vol. I covers his entire life and most of his works but contains little that is new. Its main value resides in certain perceptive observations on BI's *valencianismo*. Vol. II is a digression on Valencia's long history, by means of which Domínguez seeks to expand the definition of traditionalism so that in vol. III, when he discusses BI's early Valencian works (i.e. the repudiated as well as the recognized works) and BI's later defense of Spain against the *leyenda negra*, the reader will accept his portrayal of BI as a traditionalist, notwithstanding BI's anti-monarchism, his denial of religion, and his admiration for the French Republic. See also Bb513.

Ba26 Edel, Roger, *VBI in seinem Verhältnis zu einigen neueren französischen Romanschriftstellern*, Münster: Buchdruckerei Thiele, 1935, 121pp.
Most of this published Ph.D. dissertation (Westfälischen Wilhelms Univ.– Münster) examines the relationship between the works of BI and those of Zola. Edel finds that BI's Valencian cycle is influenced by the Rougon-Macquart series in specific scenes, its impressionist and expressionist techniques, its indirect form of narration, use of certain preferred naturalist themes, handling of symbolism, etc. Edel also discerns fundamental differences: BI is free of Zola's scientific tendencies, lacks his noble concern for mankind's material and moral betterment, and evolves as a novelist from optimism to pessimism, which is the opposite of Zola's trajectory. Edel calls BI a literary freeborrower who plagiarizes Flaubert's *Salammbô* in *Sónnica*, and both G. Rodenbach's *Bruges-la-morte* and the Goncourts' *Manette Salomon* in *La maja desnuda*. Despite its title, however, *La catedral* owes nothing to Huysmans's novel of same name.

Ba27 Los escritores españoles, *Libro-homenaje al inmortal novelista VBI*, Val.: Prometeo, 1929, 240pp.
This memorial volume has three parts:
   I. A facsimile of 'Las vírgenes locas' in the handwriting of twenty-five writers (each copied out one page); most are second-rate, but they include E. Marquina, A. Palacio Valdés, R. Pérez de Ayala. Also contains critical judgments on BI by preceding writers and R. Menéndez

Pidal, S. Ramón y Cajal, etc.

II. 'BI, novelista', 'BI, periodista', 'BI, político', 'BI y los poetas', 'BI y la juventud literaria'. Each of the five preceding categories contains between five and twelve often quite brief statements on BI as novelist, journalist, politician, etc.

III. Briefer items on miscellaneous aspects of BI's life and works by M. Domingo, E. Estevez Ortega, and others.

Because of the low quality of most items in this volume, it is of little value to scholars. Consequently, of its more than seventy entries, cross reference is made here only to the following: M. Azaña, Bb39; F. Bergamín, Bb72; R. Cansinos-Asséns, Bb106; M. Machado, Bb320; E. Marquina, Bb330; R. Menéndez Pidal, Bb350; R. Pérez de Ayala, Bb404; S. Ramón y Cajal, Bb449. See also Bb431.

Ba28   Esplá, Carlos, *Unamuno, BI y Sánchez Guerra en París*, B.A.: Ed. Araujo, 1940, 93pp.

Admiringly recounts (especially pp. 51-75) BI's return to political activity, his sacrifices and editorial efforts in Paris against Spain's dictatorship. Has interesting details on BI and Unamuno, how BI's *España con Honra* circulated clandestinely in Spain, etc.

Ba29   Fernández de García Huidobro, M. Luisa, *BI démasqué: réponse au calomniateur du roi d'Espagne.* Tr. by Marius André. Paris: Librairie M.-P. Trémois, 1925, 54pp.

Published to diminish the effect on French public opinion of BI's French-language publications against Spanish king. A typical inventory of BI's supposed vices and faults, this booklet attempts to win sympathy for Alfonso XIII by stressing his humanitarian actions in the European War.

Ba30   Fortuny, José Albert, 'Valencia en BI', Unpubl. Ph.D. dissertation, Univ. of Valencia, 1962, 883pp.

Fortuny attempts to analyse that part of BI's Valencian *costumbrismo* that corresponds to the author's creative imagination and to distinguish it from that part which reflects accurately the socio-historical realities of the Valencia of BI's own lifetime.

Ba31   Gascó Contell, Emilio, *BI*, Paris: Agencia Mundial de Librería, 1925, 208pp.

This uncritical biography tends to highlight the more adventurous, dynamic side of BI's life. As a friend of the novelist, Gascó is able to provide interesting anecdotes and personal details that are reproduced in numerous subsequent biographies. The observations on BI's novels, however, are superficial. There is also considerable plot summary of certain novels, often borrowed from Zamacois: Ba103.

Ba32   —, *BI y su obra*, Val.: Ed. Mediterráneo, 1921, 24pp.

This pamphlet, illustrated with six photographs, presents high points of BI's life and works in very general terms. Intended for a popular audience on the occasion of BI's triumphal return visit to Valencia, it contains nothing not treated more completely in Gascó's later works.

Ba33   —, *Las cuatro vidas de VBI y nuevos documentos sobre la aventura argentina, Celebridades*, Madrid (Feb. 1966), 56pp.

The entire issue of *Celebridades (Revista Popular de Biografías)* is dedicated to Gascó's study, which divides BI's life into the four customary periods. New documentation promised in title is largely a letter from Dr Gaspar Bonastre, Argentine judge, who provides some details and personal observations on BI's Nueva Valencia colony and consequent lawsuits. Gascó quotes extensively from this letter to justify BI's activities and his vision as a colonizer.

Ba34   —, *Genio y figura de BI: agitador, aventurero y novelista*, M: Afrodisio Aguado, 1957, 236pp.

Seven chapters divide BI's life into distinct periods or moments, each of which is enhanced by excellent photographs or illustrations from that period. The prefatory "Unas palabras del biógrafo" explain Gascó's affection for BI and the nature of their relationship. Seven appendices, ranging from a graphological study of BI to the reproduction of one of his public addresses, complete this work. In general, this is a useful life-study which chronicles BI's active life and also creates a clear image of the uniqueness of his personality. Like Gascó's 1925 study, Ba31, it is uncritical and surprisingly vague or incorrect with regard to many dates and bibliographical facts.

Ba35   —, *Genio y figura de VBI*, M: Afrodisio Aguado, 1967, 282pp.

A changed and shortened title, as well as a new copyright, distinguish this abbreviated pocket-book version of Gascó's 1957 study, Ba34. Although the text of the study is the same, the book lacks the earlier version's prefatory explanation, all of its illustrations, and the entire section of appendices.

Ba36   Gilbert, Donald Monroe, 'The Personal Accusative in the Works of BI', Unpubl. Ph.D. dissertation, Univ. of Wisconsin, 1920, 174pp.

No *DissA*. Reviews literature on Spanish personal accusative and establishes for it a classification of regular grammatical usage. On applying the categories of this classification to BI's prose, Gilbert concludes that the apparent irregularities or exceptions often indicate an "effort towards clearness, accuracy, euphony, etc., rather than capricious choice" on the part of the author.

Ba37 Giménez Soler, Andrés, *El carácter de don Pedro de Luna: a propósito de don VBI, 'El Papa del Mar'*, Zaragoza: Tipografía 'La Académica', 1926, 51pp.

Objective, factual and detailed examination of BI's use of historical sources in *El Papa del Mar*. Faults BI for altering historical truth by adding material or changing facts, situations, etc., to suit his particular purpose.

Ba38 Gómez Martí, Pedro, *Psicología del pueblo valenciano según las novelas de BI*, Val.: Ed. Prometeo, n.d. [1931], 286pp.

Operating on the assumption that BI's Valencian works reflect a 'realidad vivida y no modificada esencialmente', Gómez Martí examines them as documents which will shed light on the behavioral patterns, customs, beliefs, of the Valencians. He borrows freely from a broad range of scientific writings and applies those theories that will help him interpret and classify the underlying psychology of the Valencians. Although many chapters in this basically cataloging study reveal nothing that any intelligent reader could not grasp for himself, others, such as 'Alimentación', 'Psicología del sedentarismo', 'Criminalidad y alcoholismo', are well reasoned, suggestive, and contain many facts useful to the student of BI's novels.

Ba39 González-Blanco, Andrés, *VBI: juicio crítico de sus obras*, M: La Novela Corta, 1920, unpaginated (48pp).

This booklet, no. 242 in series *La Novela Corta*, treats individually and in chronological order seventeen novels. Most attention is given to the Valencian works. Although the well-known critic sometimes makes perceptive comments on BI, his study is generally unreliable. In addition to frequent inaccuracies, e.g. 'tía Picota' in *Flor de Mayo*, González-Blanco's judgments are highly subjective and he reveals a fondness for exaggeration and absolute opinions that are unsupported by the texts he frequently cites in order to prove his assertions.

Ba40 Greiner, Annedörte, *VBI: der spanische Zola?* Jena: Universitäts-Buchdruckerei G. Neuenhahn, 1932, 79pp.

In this comparison of BI and Zola (a 1931 Jena Ph.D. dissertation), the author examines successively the novels of BI's Valencian and thesis cycles. She concludes that, despite certain similarities, BI was not a naturalist in the same sense as Zola. Consequently, BI does not merit the epithet of 'the Spanish Zola'. In general, Miss Greiner's dissertation is superficial and naive. See also Ba26, Bb430.

Ba41 Greve, Gladys Adelyn, 'A Comparison between *Salammbô* by

Gustave Flaubert and *Sónnica la cortesana* by VBI', Unpubl. M.A. thesis, Univ. of Oklahoma, 1936, 63pp. *

Ba42　Grijalba, Alfonso Ruiz de, *Los enemigos del rey (al margen de una campaña)*, M: Ed. Marineda, 1924, 134pp.

Attacks Unamuno and BI as unpatriotic. Defends Alfonso XIII against slander of exiled authors. Attributes their attacks on Alfonso to Unamuno's ambition to be Minister of Education and BI's aspirations to presidency of a Spanish federal republic.

Ba43　Hamel, Bernard, 'El paisaje en BI', Unpubl. Ph.D. dissertation, Univ. of Madrid, 1962, 260pp.

This dissertation (program of doctoral studies for foreign students) examines from different perspectives BI's treatment of nature and the role of nature in his novels. Shows how nature is personified into a dynamic force, but a force that remains indifferent to man's plight in this world.

Ba44　Heartfield, Gilbert B., 'Aesthetics and Naturalism in the Five Valencian Novels of VBI', Unpubl. Ph.D. dissertation, Univ. of New Mexico, 1972, 234pp.

DissA, XXXII,11 (1972), p. 6428A. Analyses each novel from standpoint of characterization, psychology, point of view, novelistic technique, structure and time, language, naturalism, *costumbrismo*. Through the critical analysis of literary elements, Heartfield demonstrates that a close relationship exists between the novels' aesthetic qualities and the author's naturalistic outlook, particularly with regard to the expression of naturalistic pessimism through poetic and symbolic means.

Ba45　Hernández Gavira, J., *VBI en Manila*, Manila: The Times Press, 1924, 196pp.

A detailed account of BI's brief visit to the Philippines is given in this illustrated volume. Provides interesting view of Philippine welcome and BI's propaganda campaign for Hispanic culture in Spain's former colony.

Ba46　Hick, Karen, 'Anti-Progressist Characters in the Works of BI', Unpubl. M.A. thesis, Univ. of Tennessee, 1960, 40pp. *

Ba47　Just Gimeno, Juli, *BI i València*, Val.: L'estel, 1929, 121pp.

This excellent biography, written in the Valencian dialect, provides a factually accurate account of BI's first 28 years. Part I, 'Infància', is particularly valuable for details of BI's Aragonese ancestry which BI embellished or kept secret. Also covers different periods of BI's education, his readings, youthful acquaintances and heroes, and his knowledge of Valencia and its history. Part II, 'Joventut', begins with BI's university period and traces his early activities as a political agitator, winning of Valencian workers for the Republican cause, etc. This important study, much used by other biographers, is refreshing in its refusal to idolize its subject, notwithstanding Just's admiration for BI. See also Bb433.

Ba48   King, Janet Elizabeth, 'Sense, Symbol and Suggestion in Selected Novels of VBI', Unpubl. Ph.D. dissertation, Columbia Univ., 1972, 394pp. *
No *DissA.*

Ba49   Kloe, Donald Robert, 'A Critical Survey of the Novels of VBI from 1909 to 1928', Unpubl. Ph.D. dissertation, Univ. of Virginia, 1971, 187pp. *
DissA, XXXII,8 (1972), p. 4570A. Examines twelve novels written after BI's return from Argentina and establishes three major categories. Concludes that BI wrote these later novels for the world and for himself. This, he feels, accounts for the major differences between these novels and the works written prior to 1909, which were for Spain and the Spaniards.

Knowlton, E.C.: see Day, A.G.

Ba50   León Roca, F. [sic], *BI: política i periodisme*, B: Edicions 62, 1970, 186pp.
The only study focusing on BI's journalism. J.L. León Roca provides (1) an introduction to BI's total journalistic experience, (2) commentary in Catalan on anthologized selections (arranged thematically) from BI's articles in *El Pueblo* (1894-1906), (3) a listing of approximately one thousand articles by BI in *El Pueblo*. This book reveals BI as a journalist during his most active and creative period. A defect of the study is the extreme brevity of the selections. It also omits several key articles and attributes to BI certain articles signed by F. Pi y Margall.

Ba51   León Roca, J.L., *VBI*, Val.: Prometeo, 1967, 660pp.
The best study of BI's life. León Roca's knowledge of Valencian politics, history, and literature enables him to contribute valuable new information on the life of BI in his native city. For instance, the BI-Rodrigo Soriano affair is presented here with more detail than anywhere else. What is said of BI's life after 1909, however, is largely derived from earlier studies. This book is beautifully illustrated; its text incorporates information from largely inaccessible newspapers, on which it relies heavily. Like preceding studies, it stresses BI's life rather than his works, which are, with a few exceptions, not examined in depth. As with Gascó and Meliá before him, León Roca's admiration for BI at times prevents

an unbiased assessment or interpretation of BI's character or behavior.

——, see also Loubès, Ba54.

Ba52   Levi, Ezio, *VBI e il suo capolavoro 'Cañas y barro'*, Firenze: Casa Editrice 'La Voce', 1922, 46pp.

Levi observes that BI's own physical energy and mental vigor are reflected in many of his vigorous characters, who also view life as an endless struggle. Levi's most interesting ideas concern the novel's structure, which he considers to be built around three dramatic scenes (the revelation of Tonet's and Neleta's carnal love; the infanticide;Tonet's suicide), all of which take place on the Albufera. Levi says little else that is noteworthy.

Ba53   López Soler, Leandro, 'Individuo y sociedad en la Valencia de 1900 a través de las obras de BI', Unpubl. Ph.D. dissertation, Univ. of Valencia, 1971, 341pp.

Treats life of the individual, the family, and society in general in both the city and province of Valencia as seen through the novels of BI.

Ba54   Loubès, J.N., and J.L. León Roca, *VBI, diputado y novelista*, Toulouse: France-Ibérie Recherche, 1972, 178pp.

Part I traces BI's political activities from 1898 to 1908, stressing his participation as a Republican deputy in the Cortes. Part II reproduces from the *Diario de sesiones de Cortes* BI's most notable speeches in the Cortes (with excellent background material on each).

Ba55   Madrid, Francisco, *Los desterrados de la dictadura*, M: Ed. España, 1930, 261pp., especially pp. 101-91.

On BI's anti-Directory period in Paris. Provides a useful account of BI's return to politics, his polemical ability, competence in French, debate in French Parliament over Spanish government's legal charges against BI in French courts.

Ba56   Martínez de la Riva, Ramón, *BI: su vida, su obra, su muerte, sus mejores páginas*, M: Ed. Mundo Latino, 1929, 303pp.

Title accurately reflects contents of this four-part study. The first part is a factually reliable treatment of BI's life, enriched by anecdotes obtained through author's friendship with BI. The sections on BI's works and his death, however, contain little that was not already widely known about BI in 1929. The last part is an anthology of BI's works.

Ba57   Más, José, *BI y la jauría*, M: Librería A. Pueyo, 1928, 107pp.

Taking as his starting point unflattering comments of Valle-Inclán and Baroja about the recently deceased BI, Más presents a passionate defense of the Valencian author. He attributes their 'olímpico desprecio' of BI to envy of his world fame and their own total insignificance outside of Spain. Más reproduces passages from the three authors in an attempt to point out stylistic defects of Valle-Inclán and Baroja and to demonstrate BI's superior literary talent.

Ba58   Meliá Bernabeu, José [pseud: Pigmalión], *BI, novelista*, Val.: Pastor, 1963, 104pp.
See Ba59.

Ba59   ——, *BI, novelista y su universidad popular; Iturbi*, Val.: Suc. de Vives Mora - Artes Gráficas, 1967, 209pp.
'Pigmalión' prints along with his two-part 1958 London lecture on BI (which constitutes the text of his 1963 book: see Ba58), 14 previously published articles of very unequal value on BI, and a short section on the pianist Iturbi. Self-taught and unmethodical, 'Pigmalión' traces with pride his long contact with BI. He also provides some shrewd judgments on BI's character, temperament, and motivation as a politician in Valencia, a city 'Pigmalión' knows well. Unfortunately, this work's almost total absence of specific dates makes it of little use to anyone not already familiar with BI's life. The most useful of the articles concern BI's efforts on behalf of mass education, his son's library in Valencia, and 'Pigmalión's' brief secretaryship for BI.

Ba60   Miller, Michael Barry, 'A Study of Male Characterization in the Spanish Naturalistic Novel', Unpubl. Ph.D. dissertation, George Washington Univ., 1974, 217pp.
DissA, XXXV,4 (1974), p. 2285A. Discerns in three Spanish naturalistic novels (*La Regenta, Los pazos de Ulloa,* and BI's *La barraca*) a new type of male character which reflects the moral and human condition of society in the period of these novels. The male has become an antihero, the negation of the Romantic hero, and the personification of the defects of the Spanish moral, social, and religious codes. For Miller, each of the novels also reveals a world of total male dominance in which sordidness, perversity, or immorality are defining traits of important male characters.

Ba61   Miranda, Wenceslao, *Posición filosófica, religiosa y social en las novelas de tesis de BI*, Lugo: Ed. Celta, 1969, 203pp.
This study (originally an M.A. thesis, City Univ. of New York, 1968) attempts an ideological examination of BI through the analysis of four works: the thesis novels *La catedral, El intruso, La bodega,* and for contrast, *Los argonautas,* written some ten years later. Miranda, a former priest, examines the historical, philosophical, literary, and sociological influences that resulted in BI's ideological conversion to an anti-religious stance. Although BI's attack on religion is indiscriminate in nature,

Miranda recognizes the validity of some of his specific criticisms. With the passing of time, as *Los argonautas* reveals, all criticism of the Church disappears and this, for Miranda, may represent a lessening of BI's anti-clericalism and hostility towards religion.

Ba62 ——, 'Aspects of Socio-Religious Ideology in Selected Novels of BI' (text in Spanish), Unpubl. Ph.D. dissertation, Columbia Univ., 1971, 227pp. *

DissA, XXIV,12 (1974), p. 7769A. Studies the same novels as Miranda's 1969 book, Ba61, and reaches same basic conclusion, although, according to Abstract, with a sharper focus. Miranda also acclaims BI's role as an 'escritor de vigorosas ideas futuristas' because the Second Vatican Council carried out a number of the reforms he had pleaded for years before in certain thesis novels.

Ba63 Montes Huidobro, Matías, 'VBI: visión y ceguera en el estilo', ch. VI of *XIX: superficie y fondo del estilo*, Estudios de *Hispanófila*, 17, M: Castalia, 1971, pp. 83-99.

The author, who dedicates the other five chapters to Alarcón, Galdós, and Pardo Bazán, here makes stylistic observations on similar and dissimilar descriptive techniques in the initial chapter of three Valencian novels.

Ba64 Morales-Afanador, Emilia, 'Humorismo en las novelas y los cuentos de VBI', Unpubl. M.A. thesis, Univ. of Tennessee, 1960, 146pp. *

Mostacilla [pseud.]: see Navarro Cabanes, José.

Ba65 Navarro Cabanes, José [pseud: Mostacilla], *Después de leer 'Oriente'*, Val.: Imprenta M. Pau, 1908, 53pp.

Lists and comments on errors (some real, most imagined) that he finds in BI's *Oriente*. Expresses horror at BI's incorrect grammar, impossible or contradictory figures of speech, factual errors, etc.

Ba66 ——, [pseud: Un parranda], *Bajonazos al idioma*, Val.: Tipografía M. Pau, 1908, 58pp.

An ill-tempered and inane attack on *Sangre y arena*; concentrates on BI's incorrect use of Spanish, his plagiarism of other 'novelas taurinas', and the false view of Spain that he presents in this novel written to exploit a foreign reading public.

Ba67 Nicholson, Helen S., *The Novel of Protest and the Spanish Republic*, Tucson: Univ. of Arizona Bulletin, X,3 (1939), 42pp.

Author's 1935 address, the Annual Liberal Arts Lecture, is mostly an account of the contents of BI's thesis novels and how they treat social, religious, and other problems that were being resolved through reforms instituted by the Spanish Republic. Discusses works of Baroja and Pérez de Ayala in a similar way.

Ba68   Nolan, V., 'Dissertation on VBI', Unpubl. M.A. thesis, National Univ., Ireland, 1958. *

Ba69   Nunn, Marshall Elbert, 'The New BI', Unpubl. M.A. thesis, Stanford Univ., 1925. *

Ba70   Ortega, Joaquín, 'VBI', *Univ. of Wisconsin Studies in Language and Literature*, XX (1924), pp. 214-38.
Excellent essay that concentrates on BI's style, descriptive technique, impressionism. Offers a perceptive appraisal of BI's novels and points out where they differ most from Galdós's works.

Ba71   Pardales, el Doctor [pseud?], *La novela 'Sangre y arena' del señor BI ¿es una imitación de 'Niño bonito' y 'El espada', publicados en 1905 por Héctor Abreu o es una coincidencia?*, Sevilla: Tipografía de Gironés, 1908, 21pp.
An unsuccessful attempt to prove that BI plagiarized Abreu's novels.

Parranda, un [pseud.] : see Navarro Cabanes, José.

Pigmalión [pseud.] : see Meliá Bernabeu, J.M.

Ba72   Pitollet, Camille, *BI, paisajista*, Paris: Casa Ed. Vuibert, 1924, 130pp.
A selection of twenty-eight descriptive passages from BI's works. Contains introduction on BI's life and literary style and '¿No querías oír al ruiseñor? ', an essay which discusses the famous nightingale passage of *Entre naranjos* in light of similar passages in Boccaccio, Maupassant, and other European authors. This may have been designed as a text-book for a course in stylistics.

Ba73   ——, *Gloses*, Lille-Paris: V. Bresle, 1933, 314pp.
Pitollet evokes in these memoirs the Spanish men of letters he has known. Among these, BI receives by far the most attention and unfavorable commentary. Rodrigo Soriano, BI's enemy, is treated with admiration and affection. Pitollet includes in these reflections what is basically his essay, published later in Spanish, Ba74, on how he wrote his well-known study on BI. Very revealing and unflattering to BI is Pitollet's account of BI's relationship with E. Gómez Carrillo. *Gloses* also contains many useful bibliographical references and details.

Ba74   ——, 'Mi libro sobre BI', *Boletín de la Biblioteca de Menéndez*

Pelayo, XXXIII, 3-4 (1957), pp. 221-365.

In addition to reproducing extensive portions of the Spanish version of his 1921 book on BI, Ba75, Pitollet recounts somewhat bitterly the circumstances of his writing of that book. He reveals many facts about BI, who commissioned the book, exercised absolute control over its contents, translated and edited the Spanish version himself under the false name of Tulio Moncada, and failed to remunerate Pitollet as promised.

Ba75   ——, *VBI: ses romans et le roman de sa vie*, Paris: Calman-Lévy, 1921, 327pp. Spanish version: *VBI: sus novelas y la novela de su vida*, tr. by Tulio Moncada, Val.: Prometeo, 1921, 311pp.

This study, full of praise for BI's writings and other accomplishments, was in part written by BI himself: see Ba74. It consequently omits many circumstances, events, and persons that BI chose to have excluded. Despite this lack of objectivity, 'Pitollet's' attractively illustrated study contains much useful information and also sheds light on BI's own sentiments regarding his life and works. See also Bb93.

Ba76   Posada Noriega, Juan, *Las glorias del pueblo mejicano, repeliendo la agresión de BI*, Santander: Imprenta La Gráfica, 1924, 112pp. Also: México: Talleres Carlos Rivadeneyra, 1926, 132pp.

Bombastic apologia for Mexico's army, revolution, politics, great men. Attempts a point-by-point refutation of criticism in BI's *El militarismo mejicano*.

Ba77   Precioso, Artemio, 'Recuerdos de BI', in *Españoles en el destierro*, M: Ed. Vulcano, 1930, pp. 171-266.

Personal impressions and interviews with BI. Includes many letters. The admiring Precioso provides many fascinating facts about BI's character, life in France, second wife, final years of life, etc. His memoirs are a recommended source of information on BI's French period.

Ba78   Puccini, Mario, *VBI*, Roma: A.F. Formiggini, 1926, 64pp.

A small-format booklet that presents some of the basic facts on BI. It emphasizes how his temperament is reflected in his literary characters, making him an author whose life and works are genuinely inseparable.

Ba79   Quirós y Arias, Luis, *Mi homenaje a BI*, Tomelloso: Artes Gráficas, 1934, 127pp.

Quirós, a Manchegan artist who visited BI in Menton, expresses in prose and verse his admiration for the Valencian author. Although ingenuous in its praise, this work is nonetheless an interesting human document that mirrors the loyal admiration BI so often inspired in other persons.

Ba80 Revilla, Manuel G., *El novelista BI*, México: Andrés Botas e hijo, 1920, 26pp.

Reproduces Revilla's address on occasion of Univ. of Mexico's *velada* honoring BI (6.4.20). Largely superficial comments on BI's literary personality and on *Sangre y arena.*

Ba81 Ribelles Pérez, Vicente, *VBI*, 'Temas españoles', no. 480, M: Publicaciones Españolas, 1967, 41pp.

Good synthesis of BI's life but shallow discussion of his works. This pamphlet is marred by an apologia for réligion and its lamentation over BI's lack of religious faith. The seventeen photographs and even their captions are reproduced from León Roca's *VBI*, Ba51, with no acknowledgment as to their source. Moreover, much of the biographical material is borrowed from León Roca's book although his name is rarely cited and he is not given proper credit.

Ba82 Rivacoba y Rivacoba, Manuel de, *Las ideas penales de BI*, Santa Fe: Univ. Nacional del Litoral, 1966, 179pp.

This is a thoughtful and penetrating study of an overlooked aspect of BI's fictional world. Rivacoba, a former political prisoner in Spain, examines BI's dissatisfaction with the justice of his time and how this attitude is reflected in his writings. He extracts from BI's works his ideas on crime, its causes, and criminology in general. Rivacoba also classifies the criminal types portrayed in certain novels and short stories. Rivacoba concludes that although BI's 'ideas penales y criminológicas' are in themselves of no great significance or originality, their literary expression is nonetheless very powerful.

Ba83 Rosas y Reyes, Román, *Las imposturas de VBI: verdades sobre México*, B: Librería Sintes, 1922, 434pp.

A Mexican author attempts to refute BI's criticism of Mexico's revolution and politics in *El militarismo mejicano* by means of historical argument, documentary evidence, and even by personal attacks on BI's character and morals.

Ba84 Rueda, Jorge A., *Pluma falsa*, México: Imprenta Franco-mexicana, 1920, 221pp.

Subtitled 'Refutación a BI', this book is yet another effort to discredit BI and the accuracy of his account of Mexican militarism. Rueda asserts that BI's stay in Mexico was too short for him to speak authoritatively and that United States oil money motivated his attack on Mexico.

Ba85 Rueda y Maestro, Emilio de, *VBI visto a través de su obra*

(impresiones de un lector), M: Unión Poligráfica, 1935, 40pp.
Originally a lecture delivered before the Círculo Republicano Radical
de Madrid (31.5.35), this booklet offers impressionistic and personal
observations and interpretations of certain of BI's works. Rueda declares
BI's romanticism to be far more important than his naturalism. This
publication contains little of real substance.

Ba86   Sacks, Norman P., *Los chuetas de Mallorca y 'Los muertos
mandan' de BI: un capítulo en la historia de los judíos en
España*, B.A.: La Técnica Impresora, 1970, 45pp.
An impressive study of the Jewish theme and a penetrating analysis of
the concept of *limpieza de sangre* as it applies to *Los muertos mandan*.
First published with a slightly different title in *Davar*, Bb463, this
revised booklet edition of that study adds a valuable section of bibliographical and interpretative notes.

Ba87   San Román, José, *La muerte del águila: vida y recuerdos de
BI, su reivindicación y muerte*, M: Ed. Pueyo, 1928, 92pp.
On the basis of two brief visits with BI in 1922 and 1924, and from
reading his novels and works about him, San Román offers fulsome
praise of BI, describes his generous and forgiving nature, and defends
him from attacks by political enemies. San Román's work is the least
convincing of all apologias for BI.

Ba88   Santisteban, Héctor de, *BI*, B: Ediciones EP, 1959, 64pp.
Written for a popular reading public, this Enciclopedia Pulga booklet
is largely a synthesis of BI's family background, his early education, and
his university days in Valencia. Santisteban says very little about BI's
life after 1898. Moreover, he limits himself to mentioning BI's best-
known works and provides merely a one-sentence characterization of
some of these.

Ba89   Sebastià, Enric, *València en les novel·les de BI: proletariat i
burgesia*, Val.: L'estel, 1966, 127pp.
A new and suggestive approach to BI's Valencian novels. Sebastià
examines these works as socio-economic documents on restoration
Valencia. Methodically applying the theories of A. Hauser to BI's works,
Sebastià finds that they reflect faithfully the dynamic and shifting
Valencian social structure as well as such situations as the exploitation
of the proletariat by the bourgeoisie and of the countryside by the city.
See also Bb287.

Ba90   Smith, Paul C., *VBI: una nueva introducción a su vida y obra*,
Santiago: Univ. Austral de Chile and Ed. A. Bello, 1972, 45pp.
Attempts to cover concisely and analytically the fundamental informa-

tion on BI's life and works.

Ba91 ——, 'VBI: A Critical Survey of the Novels from 1894 to 1909', Unpubl. Ph.D. dissertation, Univ. of California, 1964, 270pp.
DissA, XXV,10 (1965), p. 5943. Examines fourteen novels individually and as parts of two distinct groups. Basically an esthetic consideration of BI's novels, this dissertation concentrates on style, literary technique, major and minor themes, specific borrowings from French and Spanish authors, etc.

Ba92 Sosa, Rafael, *VBI a través de sus cuentos y novelas valencianos*, M: Playor, 1974, 136pp.
Following an intrinsic approach, Sosa examines each *cuento* and discusses its structure, themes, etc. He then applies to each one a rather self-evident label: "de costumbres, de contenido psicológico, de vida marina", etc. For each novel he offers observations on narrative technique, style, themes, etc., combined with considerable plot summary. In general, this is literary criticism at an elementary level.

Ba93 Surís, Andrés, 'Técnicas cinematográficas y la obra de VBI', Unpubl. Ph.D. dissertation, Univ. of Minnesota, 1972, 213pp. *
DissA, XXXIII,6 (1972), p. 2955A. Provides a different approach to BI's later works by showing how BI gradually identified himself with the new art of the cinema in such a way that he actually created a 'novela cinematográfica'.

Ba94 Swain, James O., *VBI: General Study, Special Emphasis on Realistic Techniques*, Knoxville: Graphic Arts-Univ. of Tennessee, 1959, 180pp.
This is a slightly revised version of Swain's Ph.D. dissertation on BI's realism, Ba96. It differs from the dissertation by the addition of the section 'Twenty-five Years Later' (Swain's impressions from a 1933 visit to Spain) and the inclusion of two articles published in *Hispania*: Bb497; Bb498.

Ba95 ——, 'The Realism of VBI', Unpubl. M.A. thesis, Indiana Univ., 1923, 58pp. *

Ba96 ——, 'VBI—Exponent of Realism', Ph.D. dissertation, Univ. of Illinois, 1932. *
No *DissA*. (The following is taken from a printed Abstract, Urbana, 1932, 20pp., of the preceding dissertation.) In the three parts of his dissertation, Swain (1) establishes criteria for defining realism on the basis of practices and theories of Stendhal, Flaubert, and certain contemporary authors, (2) traces these criteria through BI's works to

determine to what degree they guide BI, (3) studies BI's esthetic theories to ascertain his literary ideals. Swain finds that BI is a realist of the first rank in his ability to perceive, careful observation, and the avoidance of the exotic. However, he falls short of perfection as a realist in his inability to use only significant detail. As for objectivity, BI also fails in those novels where he preaches or sustains a thesis. See also Ba94.

Ba97   Thous, Gaspar, *'Entre naranjos' o desaliños literarios de BI*, Val.: Imprenta de F. Martínez Andreu, 1901, 31pp.

Attacks idolatry of BI's person in Valencia. Sarcastic comments on *Entre naranjos*. Censures its lack of moral standards, repetition of certain adjectives, incorrect grammar, defective imagery.

Ba98   Tortosa, Pilar, *Tres mujeres en la vida y la obra de VBI*, Val.: Prometeo, 1972, 261pp.

The three parts of this study by BI's daughter-in-law deal with Ramona (BI's mother), María (his first wife), and Elena (his second wife). The book often digresses from its expressed subject, and its first two parts depend heavily on León Roca's biography, Ba51, for much information. Part III, however, provides more new details on BI's long relationship with Elena Ortúzar Bulnes than does any other work. Nonetheless, truly intimate or shocking matters are omitted or glossed over.

Ba99   Vergara Vicuña, Federico, *BI, la vuelta al mundo en 80.000 . . . dóllars*, Paris: Imprimerie Tancrède, 1924, 62pp.

Vergara writes one of the most clever published attacks on BI. Concentrating on BI's financial success and commercial instincts, Vergara combines truths, half-truths, lies, and exaggerations skillfully to create the image of an opportunistic writer and politician whose supposed political idealism and propaganda for Hispanic culture were in fact motivated by the expectation of financial gain.

Ba100   Vogt, Verne Lyle, 'Influences of Materialistic Ideas in the Novels of BI', Unpubl. Ph.D. dissertation, Univ. of Kansas, 1966, 139pp.

DissA, XXVII,6 (1966), pp. 1841-2A. Examines the influence of naturalist materialism as reflected in BI's ideas on religion, the supernatural, science, and the theory of determinism. Concludes that BI never completely abandons materialist views, although by 1916 he ceases to propagandize for such views. Despite this ideology, BI makes much of his literature serve idealistic, humanitarian purposes.

Ba101   XX y X . . . [pseud.], *La verdad sobre la cuestión Blasco-Soriano*, Val.: Imprenta de *El Radical*, 1903, 128pp.

Details the development of BI's relationship with Rodrigo Soriano and their falling out in 1903. Provides specifics on Soriano's loan to BI, dishonesty of BI's father, etc. This book written by a friend (or friends) of Soriano covers much the same material that was printed in Soriano's Valencian daily, *El Radical*, during the early stages of their feud. For balance, it should be read in conjunction with the more vituperative opposing view presented in BI's own paper, *El Pueblo*.

Ba102 Xandró, Mauricio, *BI*, M: Ediciones y Publicaciones Españolas, 1971, 196pp.

This mixture of personal commentary and information drawn largely from Gascó Contell, Pitollet, and BI's own statements and works, is, regrettably, published in a well-known series (Grandes Escritores Contemporáneos , no. 39). Xandró's inadequate preparation for his task is apparent in frequent bibliographical and factual inaccuracies as well as ignorance. Of BI's first wife, for example, Xandró writes: "luego desaparece de su vida, sin que podamos saber si muere o es abandonada", p. 30. Xandró includes a graphological and physiognomic interpretation of BI as well as an anthology of passages from his writings.

Ba103 Zamacois, Eduardo, *Mis contemporáneos*, I. *VBI*, M: Librería Sucesores de Hernando, 1910, 119pp.

The six chapters of this earliest of all major studies on BI analyse the works written from 1894 until BI's departure for Argentina. Especially revealing are Zamacois's portrait of the author at work in Madrid and the confessions about life and love which BI makes to his friend, Zamacois. BI's novels are intelligently reviewed and Zamacois also isolates certain constants in BI's works and discusses distinct types of women characters in his fiction. See also Ba104.

Ba104 ——, *VBI*, M: La Novela Mundial, 1928, 122pp.

Only the addition of ch. VII, highlights of BI's life and works from his return from Argentina in 1914 until his death in 1928, distinguishes this homage volume of 'La Novela Mundial' from its 1910 predecessor. See Ba103.

ARTICLES, LESS SUBSTANTIAL PARTS OF BOOKS, OTHER REFERENCES, etc.

Bb1 Aguilar, Mario, 'BI, cinematografista', *El Imparcial* (2.8.16).
D'Annunzio's influence on BI's film-making career; BI's first production, *Sangre y arena*; his plans for film *Don Quijote*.

Bb2 Alas, Leopoldo [pseud: Clarín], *Pluma y lápiz* (24.2.01). *
BI 'tiene condiciones de novelista digno de ser leído'. Cited by S. Beser in *Leopoldo Alas, crítico literario*, p. 311.

Bb3 Alcalá Galiano, Alvaro, 'BI en Mentón', *ABC* (1.4.22).
Interview: author's working habits, villa, isolation from visitors.

Bb4 ——, 'La gloria de BI', *EP* (29.10.33).
BI's appearance, character, friendship for AAG.

Bb5 ——, 'La gloria y la muerte: impresiones', *ABC* (1.2.28).
BI's plans shortly prior to his death.

Bb6 ——, 'Torcuato Luca de Tena o el periodista patriota', in *Figuras excepcionales*, M: Renacimiento, 1930, pp. 210-12.
TLT defends Sp. monarchy from BI's criticism during formal dinner.

Bb7 ——, 'Un novelista mundial, BI', in *Figuras excepcionales*, M: Renacimiento, 1930, pp. 53-63.
BI's life and literary achievements.

Bb8 Alfonso, José, 'BI' in *Siluetas literarias*, Val.: Prometeo, 1967, pp. 57-9.
Meetings between the young J. Alfonso and BI.

Bb9 ——, 'BI, V', in *Siluetas literarias*, Val.: Prometeo, 1967, pp. 193-5.
How BI refused to follow literary fashion.

Bb10 Almela y Vives, Francisco, 'Aniversario del gran novelista valenciano: relaciones de BI con el teatro', *Mundo Gráfico* (26.1.32).
BI's unfinished play *Guillem Sorolla* and completed play *El juez*.

Bb11 ——, 'Vida y muerte de BI', *Levante: Suplemento Gráfico de los Domingos*, Val. (29.1.67).
Concise sketch of BI's life.

Bb12 Alomar, Gabriel, 'La estela de BI', *Repertorio Americano*, XVI,13 (1928), 203.
Despite excellent early novels, BI's person 'descollará por encima de su obra entera'.

Bb13 Alonso, Martín, in *Evolución sintáctica del español*, M: Aguilar, 1964, pp. 329, 336-41.
Samples of BI's prose arranged in syntactic categories.

Bb14 Alpera, Juan F., 'El paisaje en la obra de BI', *Las Provincias*, Val. (29.1.67).
Subjective comments on BI's stylistic treatment of Valencian milieu.

Bb15 Altamira, Rafael, 'A propósito de BI', *La Nación*, B.A. (11.3.28).
Recalls university years with BI. Several facts not given elsewhere.

Bb16 ——, 'BI, novelista', in *Arte y realidad*, B: Cervantes, 1921, pp. 115-24.
Characteristics of earliest Valencian works; BI's style.

Bb17 ——, 'La novela valenciana', *Revista Crítica de Historia y Literatura*, I (June-July 1896), 258-61.
Praises *costumbrismo* in *Arroz y tartana*, *Flor de Mayo* but censures coarse, offensive scenes.

Bb18 ——, 'Una novela sobre la guerra', in *Arte y realidad*, B: Cervantes, 1921, pp. 125-30.
On epic qualities of *Cuatro jinetes del Apocalipsis.*

Bb19 Amade, Jean, 'L'Évolution d'un romancier valencien', in *Études de littérature méridionale*, Toulouse: Privat-Paris: Picard, 1907, pp. 21-61.
Asserts novels of social thesis represent the decadence of BI's art.

Bb20 Anderson Imbert, Enrique, 'VBI', in *El cuento español*, B.A.: Columba, 1959, pp. 30-1.
Enumerates main characteristics of BI's short stories.

Andrenio [pseud.]: see Gómez de Baquero, Eduardo.

Bb21 Aníbal, C.E., 'BI', *Hispania* (USA), XII,4 (1929), 421-5.
Reprints and comments on BI's autobiographical letter first published by C. Pitollet; see Bb423 and Ad3.

Bb22   Antoine, M., 'L'Exploitation d'une carrière, BI', *Le Correspondant*, Paris, CCCX, 1570 (1928), 590-9.
BI's temperament; BI as a publicist of own enterprises; how he compromised Franco-Spanish diplomatic relations; French translations of BI's works are actually shortened adaptations, etc.

Bb23   Araceli, Gabriel, 'Ante una decoración de *El Papa del mar*: los hombres de lucha en las novelas de BI', *Nuevo Mundo* (3.6.27).
View of Peñíscola; commentary on novel's protagonist.

Bb24   Aramburu, Juan, 'Cartas de París: BI y el cinematógrafo', *El Día Gráfico* (28.12.27).
BI's novels are easily adapted to motion pictures; why BI prefers films to the theater.

Bb25   Araujo, Fernando, 'Literatura', *La España Moderna*, XV,4 (1903), 170-2.
Discusses comments on BI included in C. Pitollet's inaugural lecture as professor in Hamburg.

Bb26   Araujo-Costa, Luis, 'Autores y libros: *La vuelta al mundo de un novelista*', *La Época* (23.9.25).
Long, favorable review.

Bb27   ——, 'La nueva novela de BI: *A los pies de Venus*', *La Época* (29.1.27).
On BI's new method of writing historical novels; criticizes certain omissions.

Bb28   ——, 'Un nuevo libro de BI', *La Época* (13.12.27).
Review: *Novelas de amor y de muerte*.

Bb29   Arazo, María Angeles, 'En el centenario de BI: diálogo con el nieto del gran novelista', *Levante*, Val. (29.1.67).
Vicente Blasco-Ibáñez Tortosa, BI's grandson and director of revived Ed. Prometeo, discusses events of BI centennial.

Bb30   Arcadio [pseud.], 'Glosas del día: BI y la nueva generación', *EP* (4.2.28).
How reactions in Spain and abroad among young literary generations differ regarding BI.

Bb31   Arciniega, R., 'Un gran novelista silenciado', *El Universal*, Caracas (13.11.58). *

Bb32   Argente, Baldomero, '*La horda* por BI', *EP* (22.7.05).
Penetrating review.

Bb33   Argilés, Lucas, 'BI de viaje: del vapor al tren', *El Liberal*
(18.11.12).
BI speaks of his life in Argentina.

Bb34   Arlandis, Lisard, 'BI, mantenedor de los Juegos Florales',
Las Provincias, Val. (29.1.67).
BI and 1891 Jochs Florals in Valencia.

Bb35   Armiñán, Luis de, 'El duelo de Blasco y Alastuei', *Informaciones* (28.1.28).
Details on BI's most publicized duel.

Bb36   Asociación patronal de las artes del libro en Valencia, *La
Semana BI*, Val., 1921. *
Several photographs and summary of daily activities during Valencia's
week of homage to BI.

Bb37   Astín, Claudio, 'Frente al Mare Nostrum: *Chimo y Visentico*',
Informaciones (28.1.28).
Explains inspiration of BI's 'Impunidad'.

Bb38   Aubrun, Charles V., '*Cañas y barro* de BI: Sens et formes;
structure et signification', in *Litterae Hispanae et Lusitanae:
Festschrift zum Fünfzigjährigen Bestehen des Ibero-Amerikanischen Forschungsinstituts der Universität Hamburg*,
München: Max Hueber, 1968, pp. 43-57.
Wide-ranging perceptive judgments on this novel; reveals its structural
similarities to *The Odyssey*.

Bb39   Azaña, Manuel, in Ba27, p. 76.
Calls BI a great novelist and his *La barraca* and *Cañas y barro* true
masterpieces.

Bb40   Aznar, Manuel, 'La España de hoy: BI', *Diario de la Marina*,
La Habana (29.1.28).
Analyses BI as a unique, significant literary figure.

Azorín [pseud.] : see Martínez Ruiz, José.

Bb41   Azzati, Felix, 'El alma de BI', *EP* (19.3.06).
BI will continue Republican struggle despite resignation from Congress.

Bb42   —— , 'BI ha muerto', *EP* (29.1.28).
Meaning of BI's life by his successor as director of *EP*.

Bb43   —— , '*La bodega*', *La Barraca*, Val. (4.3.05).
Proclaims superiority of *La bodega* and all of BI's writings to works
of Rodrigo Soriano.

Bb44 —— , 'En nuestro sitio', *EP* (17.3.06).
Reviews BI's career as deputy.

Bb45 —— , ' ¡Viva BI!', *EP* (11.12.06).
On BI's being named member of Legion of Honour.

Bb46 B., J.E., 'Anécdotas de BI', *La Nación*, B.A. (26.10.33).
Mainly BI's life up to 1905.

Bb47 Baget, F., 'Colón, según BI', *El Diluvio* (28.3.29).
How *En busca del Gran Kan* attacks myths about Columbus.

Bb48 Baig Baños, Aurelio, 'Un 'lobo de mar', de BI, fue verdadero paladín de carne y hueso', *Nuevo Mundo* (24.8.28).
BI based Capt. Llovet of 'Un lobo de mar' on Valencian Eugenio Viñes.

Bb49 Bailey, Beatrice, 'Cave-man stuff', *New York Times* (3.3.20).
Mocks in witty poem BI's controversial assertion in American lecture tour that American women prefer rough lovers.

Bb50 Ballester Soto, V., 'Impresiones literarias: *La maja desnuda*', *EP* (18.5.06).
Book's pessimism, tedium of life are common to BI's other works.

Bb51 Balseiro, José, 'VBI: hombre de acción y de letras', *Puerto Rico*, San Juan, I,1 (April 1935), 1-23.
Rambling essay on BI's powers of observation, eventful life, etc.

Bb52 Bardi, Ubaldo, 'VBI e l'Italia', *Les Langues Néo-Latines*, 180 (April 1967), 31-5.
Lists Italian translations of BI's works.

Bb53 Barga, Corpus [pseud. of Andrés García de la Barga] ,'BI y el cinematógrafo', *La Nación*, B.A. (29.7.34).
Unusual circumstances of second contract for film rights of *Los cuatro jinetes del Apocalipsis*.

Bb54 —— , 'BI y Unamuno en París', *Ínsula*, 250 (Sept. 1967), 1,14 and cont. in 251 (Oct. 1967), 5,11.
Authors' conversations on Primo de Rivera; their friendship, rivalry, incompatible natures.

Bb55 Barja, César, 'VBI', in *Libros y autores modernos*, New York: Las Américas, 1964, pp. 391-414.
Excellent survey of life and works.

Bb56 Baroja, Pío, 'BI', in *OC*, vol. V, M: Biblioteca Nueva, 1948, pp. 796-81.
Unfavorable impressions of BI; lists four occasions authors met.

Bb57 ——, in *Galería de tipos de la época*, *OC*, vol. VII, M: Biblioteca Nueva, 1949, pp. 869-74.
Negative comments on BI going back to first meeting in 1892. Baroja's most extensive statement on BI.

Bb58 ——, 'Gente de las afueras', *Ahora*, M. (6.3.33).
Baroja's own *La busca*, *Mala hierba*, *Aurora roja* show authentic interest in Madrid's 'afueras'. BI's *La horda* imitates them but has 'aire industrial y vulgar de casi todo lo escrito por el novelista valenciano'.

Bb59 ——, in *Páginas escogidas*, M: Calleja, 1918, p. 148.
BI's *La horda* is 'ramplón', has artificial unity and imitates Baroja's own method of composition.

Bb60 ——, 'La supuesta generación de 1898', in *OC*, vol. V, M: Biblioteca Nueva, 1948, p. 497.
Baroja is not interested in BI's works but still wonders why he is excluded from the Generation of 1898.

Bb61 —— , *Informaciones* (28.1.28).
Untitled interview. Baroja was never BI's friend, disliked his works. At the most BI represented the Spanish Mediterranean novel.

Bb62 Battle, Carlos de, 'BI', *El Heraldo de Madrid* (9.9.20). English tr. in *The Living Age* (30.10.20).
Spain downgrades her own authors whenever foreigners praise them.

Bb63 Bell, Aubrey F.G., in *Contemporary Spanish Literature*, New York: A. Knopf, 1925, pp. 90-6.
Good general introduction to BI.

Bb64 Bellessort, André, 'Les Littératures étrangères: BI', *Revue Bleue*, LIX,13 (1921), 454-8.
BI's forte is realism; he fails when he follows French naturalism as in *Cañas y barro*.

Bb65 Benavente, Jacinto, 'De sobremesa', *Los Lunes de 'El Imparcial'* (22.3.09).
On BI's forthcoming lecture tour in B.A.

Bb66 —— , 'De sobremesa', *El Imparcial* (9.8.10).
BI's return to Argentina; his book *Argentina y sus grandezas*.

Bb67 Benavente, Luis, 'BI, historiador', *La Época* (22.4.29).
En busca del Gran Kan demonstrates BI's shift from novelist to historian.

Bb68 Benchley, Robert C., 'Anti-Ibáñez', in *Love Conquers All*, New York: Garden City Publishing Co., 1922, pp. 231-5.
Strongly criticizes BI and his American success.

Bb69   Benlliure y Tuero, Mariano, '*A los pies de Venus* por BI', *El Liberal* (28.1.27).
Explains literary techniques and treatment of history in this novel.

Bb70   ——, 'Crítica literaria: nuestra literatura en el extranjero', *El Liberal* (21.12.24).
Defends desire of Spanish authors like BI to be known abroad. Scorns J.M. Carretero's attack on BI.

Bb71   ——, 'Una novela de BI: *El Papa del mar*', *El Liberal* (14.2.26).
On BI's achievement in harmonizing two plots with different time levels.

Bb72   Bergamín, Francisco, in Ba27, p.77.
Considers BI to be greatest of contemporary Spanish novelists.

Bb73   Besteiro, Julián, '*Cañas y barro* por VBI', *El Liberal* (24.4.03).
Studies novel's action and setting.

Bb74   Betancort, José, 'Cosmopolitanismo literario: la segunda etapa de BI', *La Vanguardia* (15.8.24).
How BI evolves from a regional to a national and then to a cosmopolitan novelist.

Bb75   Betancort Cabrero, José, in *Efemérides*, Las Palmas (2.10.03). *
Essay on BI cited in Bb387, p.133.

Bb76   Betoret-París, Eduardo, 'El caso BI', *Hispania* (USA), LII,1 (1969), 97-102.
BI's religious, political ideas still affect critical judgment of his works.

Bb77   —— , 'Mito, leyenda e historia en "El último león", de BI', *Duquesne Hispanic Review*, X,3 (Winter 1971), 139-64.
Carefully traces different sources of BI's short story and analyses literary techniques used by the author.

Bb78   ——, 'Valencian Professional Types in the Works of VBI', *Kentucky Foreign Language Quarterly*, XI,2 (1964), 61-70.
General comments on representative professional types in several Valencian novels and stories.

Bb79   Billy, André, *L'Oeuvre* (29.1.28). *
Cited by C. Pitollet in Ba73, p.292. BI lacks Zola's 'densité' but he surpasses Daudet through 'la force du verbe et l'ampleur de la vision'.

Bb80   Blanco Aguinaga, Carlos, 'BI: una historia de la revolución española y la novela de una revuelta andaluza', in *Juventud del 98*, M: Siglo Veintiuno de España, 1970, pp. 189-228.
Important essay on BI and Generation of 1898; analysis of *Historia de*

la revolución española; examination of *La bodega* and *La horda* from socio-political point of view.

Bb81   Blanco-Fombona, Rufino, 'BI, buen ejemplar de humanidad', in *El espejo de tres faces*, Santiago: Ercilla, 1937, pp. 135-7.
Removal of BI's mortal remains to Valencia signified recognition of his great humanity.

Bb82   ——, 'Proclama de BI a los filipinos', in *La espada del Samuray*, M: Mundo Latino, 1924, pp. 345-50.
How BI's unpleasant Mexican and Cuban experiences determined his behavior in Manila.

Bb83   Blasco, Mariano, 'Hablando con BI', *El Día Gráfico* (21.6.15).
BI denies rumor he will return to politics and compromise Spain's neutrality.

Bb84   Bobadilla, Emilio [pseud: Fray Candil], 'Emigrantes literarios', in *Bulevar arriba, bulevar abajo*, Paris: P. Ollendorff, n.d., pp. 217-21.
Literature is merely a business for BI.

Bb85   Bonafoux, Luis, 'BI', in *Los españoles en París*, Paris: Louis-Michaud, 1912, pp. 54-6.
Changes wrought in BI by life in Argentina.

Bb86   ——, 'París al día: Blasco y Soriano', *El Heraldo de Madrid* (22.3.1900).
How BI saved Rodrigo Soriano from a French mob.

Bb87   Bonet, Román, 'BI', in *Celebridades contemporáneas*, M: F. Beltrán, n.d., pp. 34-5.
Verse sketch along with cartoon of BI.

Bb88   Bordeux, Vahdah Jeanne, 'The Decadence of Modern Spain', *The Sphere*, London, CX,1440 (1927), 329.
Details BI's indictment of Spanish monarchy and dictatorship; based largely on interview.

Bb89   Borrán, José, *España entre dos libelos*, New York: Publicidad Hispánica, 1925, 3-4; 54; 89-100.
Borrán publishes together under above title BI's *Una nación secuestrada* and J.M. Carretero's *El novelista que vendió a su patria* and then asserts that Spain's future belongs neither to BI's republic nor to Carretero's monarchy but rather to Spain's workers and intellectuals.

Bb90   Borrás, Tomás, 'Dos centenarios: los de Linares Rivas y BI', *El*

Libro Español, X,110 (1967), 83-7.
Why Linares's plays are no longer presented but BI's works continue to be read.

Bb91 Bosch, Rafael, in *La novela española del siglo XX*, I, New York: Las Américas, 1970, pp. 112-28; 195-206.
Also minor references to BI in vol. II (1971). At times stimulating and original observations on BI, but more often unimaginative or exaggerated Marxist interpretations of novels.

Bb92 —— , 'Sociologia e estética na obra de BI', *Península*, Lisboa, 5 (Dec. 1970), 36-41.
BI creates Spanish novel of social realism.

Bb93 Boussagnol, G., 'Camille Pitollet, *VBI. Ses romans et le roman de sa vie*', *Bulletin Hispanique*, XXIV,4 (1922), 393-6.
Important review of Pitollet's famous biography of BI. Points out Pitollet's changing attitude to BI. See Ba75.

Bb94 Boynton, H.W., 'A Winter Crop of Novels', *Outlook*, CXLV,8 (1927), 248.
Observations on *El Papa del mar*.

Bb95 Brousson, Jean-Jacques, in *Anatole France Abroad*, tr. by J. Pollock, New York: R.M.McBride, 1928, pp. 301-2, 331. French original: *Itinéraire de Paris à Buenos Ayres*, Paris: G. Cres, 1927.
Interesting details about competition of Anatole France and BI on Argentine lecture tour.

Bb96 Brown, Donald Fowler, 'BI, V', *New Catholic Encyclopedia*, vol. II, New York: McGraw-Hill, 1967, pp. 605-6.
Summarizes life and themes of best-known works: dismisses BI's anti-clerical novels as being of little interest.

Bb97 Bru y Vidal, Santiago, 'De *Sónnica* a *Roméu*', *Las Provincias*, Val. (29.1.67).
Discusses similarities between BI's two works which have Sagunto for setting.

Bb98 Brun, Charles, 'BI', *Les Nouvelles Littéraires*, VI (4.2.28). *

Bb99 Buceta, Erasmo, 'El origen de un cuento de BI', *Boletín de la Academia Española*, XX (1933), 93-6.
BI's 'Compasión' reflects account of a suicide reported in French press.

Bb100 Bueno, Javier, 'Tartarín con poncho', in *Mi viaje a América*,

Paris: Garnier, 1913, pp. 179-82.
Satire of BI in Argentina.

Bb101 Bueno, Manuel, 'BI', *El Liberal* (29.5.05).
BI's novels of combat serve noble social cause.

Bb102 Bulnes, Gonzalo, 'BI', *El Mercurio*, Santiago-Valparaíso
(13.11.09).
Discusses BI's literary skills. Advises Chileans to disregard unfavorable
rumors about BI and to receive him as important artist and thinker.

Caballero Audaz, el [pseud.] See Carretero, J.M.

Bb103 Cadenas, José Juan, 'Novelistas españoles: BI en Madrid', *EP*
(4.7.05).
S. Feldmann's article on BI in Berlin newspaper will assure success of
his works in German translation. See also Bb188.

Bb104 Campoy, Antonio Manuel, 'VBI, 1867-1967', *La Estafeta
Literaria*, 363 (1967), 10-11.
Indicates which of BI's novels are read in Soviet Union and why. Percep-
tive contrast of BI and Azorín .

Candil, Fray [pseud.] See Bobadilla, Emilio.

Bb105 Candamo, Bernardo G. de, '*Sangre y arena*: verdad y
documentación', *EP* (15.5.08).
Analysis of novel; how its descriptive technique captures essence of
'corrida'.

Bb106 Cansinos-Asséns, Rafael, in Ba27, pp. 88-90.
Discusses novels *Sangre y arena* and *La catedral.*

Bb107 —, *La Libertad* (15.10.26). *
Essay on *La catedral.*

Bb108 —, '*Luna Benamor* de BI', in *Los judíos en la literatura
española*, B.A.: Columna, 1937, pp. 119-26.
Setting is best part of novel; BI is unsympathetic towards the Jews.

Bb109 Carayon, Jean, 'A propos d'un livre sur BI', *Revue de
l'Enseignement des Langues Vivantes*, Paris, XXXIX (1922),
69-74. *

Bb110 Caro Baroja, Julio, in *Los Baroja*, M: Taurus, 1972, p. 130.
Pío Baroja would speak of BI, Galdós, and Palacio Valdés 'y no con
ternura'.

Bb111 —, in *Los judíos en la España moderna y contemporánea*,

vol. III, M: Arión, 1961, pp. 208-9.
Claims BI was sympathetic towards the Jews.

Bb112 Carretero, José María [pseud: el Caballero Audaz], 'BI', in *Lo que sé por mí: confesiones del siglo*, 2nd series, M: Calleja, 1922, pp. 161-74.
Interview (1915?) with BI on his youth, political experiences, European War.

Bb113 ——, 'VBI', in *Galería*, vol. I, M: Ed. Caballero Audaz, 1946, pp. 541-8.
Interview: Spain's neutrality; BI's educational and literary background. Important details about Carretero's enmity for BI.

Bb114 Carsi, A., 'VBI', *Temas (Revista Ilustrada)*, New York, VI,27 (1953). *

Bb115 Casal, Conde de, 'BI y las novelas de la guerra', *Raza Española*, III,33 (1921), 41-4.
BI masterfully depicts French 'patriotismo laico manchado por repugnante sensualismo'. Laments BI's extreme anti-German attitude; praises his portrayal of renewal of French religious faith during War.

Bb116 Casañ, J., 'El año artístico-literario en Valencia, 1890', *Revista Contemporánea*, LXXVII,343 (1890), 461.
Strengths and weaknesses of the young BI's *Caerse del cielo*.

Bb117 Casares, Julio, '*Los cuatro jinetes del Apocalipsis*, por VBI', in *Crítica efímera*, vol. II, M: Espasa-Calpe, 1944, pp. 89-92.
Attacks novel's anti-German bias. See also Bb408.

Bb118 ——, '*La tierra de todos*, por VBI', in *Crítica efímera*, vol. II, M: Espasa-Calpe, 1944, pp. 93-8.
Novel is 'clásico episodio de cine'; interview with BI on experiences in USA.

Bb119 Cassou, Jean, 'BI', *Nouvelle Revue Française*, XXX (1928), 408-9.
Vigor and force characterize BI's life.

Bb120 ——, 'Un Indépendant: BI', in *Panorama de la littérature espagnole contemporaine*, Paris: Kra, 1929, pp. 109-17.
On BI's dynamic life; why outside of Spain he is the symbol of modern Spanish literature.

Bb121 Castro, Cristóbal de, 'BI', in *Número Índice*, M: 1916, pp. 16-17.
Prose sketch of BI and caricature drawn by Fresno. Although no pub-

lisher is indicated, booklet is apparently an index of contributors to *La Novela Corta*.

Bb122 ——, 'BI o el español universal', in *Vidas fértiles*, M: Castro, 1932, pp. 170-5.
BI's life and travels make him the universal Spaniard. Refutes those who deny BI's patriotism.

Bb123 ——, 'In memoriam . . . VBI, el español universal', *Nuevo Mundo*, 1776 (3.2.28), 13 pages (unpaginated), 25 photographs.
Review of BI's life and works.

Bb124 Castrovido, Roberto, 'Charla de la semana: VBI', *EP* (5.2.28).
Recalls close friendship with BI.

Bb125 ——, 'Otra novela póstuma de BI', *Cervantes*, La Habana, I (1931), 15. *
Review: *El fantasma de las alas de oro*.

Bb126 ——, 'VBI: comprensión y silencio', *Gaceta Literaria* (15.2.28).
Although young men of letters do not read BI's works, they should try to understand why he made such an impact.

Bb127 Cavia, Mariano de, 'La horda de dentro', *EP* (1.7.05).
BI reveals 'la horda hambrienta . . . que circunda a Madrid' but 'la horda de dentro', the parasites, swindlers, tax collectors, should be subject of his next novel.

Bb128 Cejador y Frauca, Julio, in *Historia de la lengua y literatura castellana*, vol. IX, M: Revista de Archivos, Bibliotecas y Museos, 1918, pp. 467-80.
Evaluates BI's art. Reproduces BI's letter on what he feels novel should be.

Bb129 Chalon, Jean, 'Les Français à Valencia: soldes et tribunaux', *Le Figaro Littéraire* (28.7.66).
Claims Valencians today think of BI as political agitator rather than a writer.

Bb130 Chamberlin, Vernon A., 'Las imágenes animalistas y el color rojo en *La barraca*', *Duquesne Hispanic Review*, VI,2 (Fall 1967), 23-36.
BI's comparisons of persons with animals; symbolic use of red to highlight emotions.

Bb131 Charensol, Georges, 'Chez BI à Menton', *Les Nouvelles Littéraires*, 4 (14.3.25). Eng. tr. in *The Living Age* (9.5.25).
BI's comments on French authors, especially Anatole France.

Bb132 Cheyne, G.J.G., ed. of *La barraca*, London: Harrap, 1964, pp. 9-18.
Introduction to BI's life, works, and *La barraca.*

Bb133 Chumillas, Ventura, 'Por haber elogiado a BI', in *Literatos y tópicos españoles*, B.A.: Nieto, 1924, pp. 131-5.
Author denies accusations that he is a liberal priest just because he prefers works of BI to those of Valle-Inclán.

Bb134 Cintora, José, 'El camino ascendente que siguió BI', *El Liberal* (1.11.33).
Both BI's political and literary activities reveal ascending progression towards universality.

Clarín [pseud.] See Alas, Leopoldo.

Bb135 Coca, Joaquín, 'Los revolucionarios', *El Productor*, B (8.2.02).
Reveals Anarchist paper's scorn for Republicans BI and Rodrigo Soriano.

Bb136 Cola, Julio, *La ruta de los conquistadores*, M: Ambos Mundos, 1923, 152pp.
In Cola's novel, the character Martín Yáñez, Spanish novelist who founds Argentine agricultural colony of Nuevo Levante, is a transparent literary recreation of BI.

Bb137 Colburn, Guy Blandin, '*En busca del Gran Kan*', *Hispania* (USA), XII,4 (1929), 533-4.
Work is more history than literature.

Bb138 Conte, Rafael, 'VBI: lecciones de un centenario', *Cuadernos Hispanoamericanos*, 216 (1967), 507-20.
BI's unwarranted reputation as a radical still prevents a fair appraisal of his writings. He was in fact a bourgeois Republican whose demagogic oratory did not accurately reflect his true beliefs.

Bb139 Cooley, James M.L., '*Novelas de amor y de muerte*', *Books Abroad*, II,2 (1928), 40.
Reviews plot and themes of six pieces in collection.

Bb140 Corbett, Elizabeth, 'VBI Was a Utopian Reformer', *New York Times Book Review* (5.2.28).
BI always sought a cause to preach in his novels. In many ways he resembled V. Hugo.

Bb141 Cossío, Francisco de, in *Confesiones: mi familia, mis amigos y mi época*, M: Espasa-Calpe, 1959, pp. 237; 257-70; 345.
Mainly BI in France from 1924 onward. Revealing anecdotes.

Bb142 —, 'La última batalla que ha de ganar BI', *EP* (2.11.33).
BI's struggle for a republic of all the Spaniards is about to be won.

Bb143 Costa, Carlos, '*La bodega*: última novela de BI', *La Publicidad* (4.4.05).
Stresses power and truth of BI's vision of the *latifundio*.

Bb144 —, '*El intruso*: novela de VBI', *La Publicidad* (4.7.04).
Demonstrates why this thesis novel is 'de tanta actualidad'.

Bb145 —, 'La última novela de BI: *La catedral*', *La Publicidad* (5.12.03).
Considers this perhaps BI's most personal novel.

Bb146 Couffon, Claude, 'Cuando Miguel Ángel Asturias se entrevistaba con Miguel de Unamuno y VBI', *Papeles de Son Armadans*, 185-6 (1971), 401-23.
Paris interview of 1924. BI attacks Alfonso XIII and Primo de Rivera.

Bb147 Cucó Giner, Alfons, ed. of BI's *Narracions valencianes*, Ac129, pp. 5-19.
General introduction to BI's early pieces published in Valencian.

Bb148 —, 'Polèmica amb el blasquisme', in *El valencianisme polític 1874-1936*, Val.: Col·lecció Garbí, 1971, pp. 51-64.
BI's relationship to Lerroux's radicalism; BI's opposition to Solidaridad Catalana and the Valencian cultural movement. See also Bb358.

Bb149 —, 'Sobre el radicalismo valenciano', *Hispania*, M, XXIX, 111 (1969), 117-29.
Traces evolution of the Valencian Republican coalition from its creation by BI in 1896 to its disappearance in 1936.

Bb150 Curros Vázquez, Adelardo, 'Crónica: *La horda*', *EP* (3.7.05).
Stresses bitter impression novel makes on its readers.

Bb151 Dalmau Canet, S., 'El hombre del día: VBI', *Puerto Rico*, San Juan, I,8 (Dec. 1919), 228-35.
On BI's republicanism; poetic nature of his novels, etc.

Bb152 Darío, Rubén, 'La literatura española en Francia', in *Escritos dispersos*, La Plata: Univ. Nacional de la Plata, 1968, p.340.
Only Spanish author that the French wish to read in translation is BI.

Bb153 ——, in 'Novelas y novelistas', *OC*, vol. II, M: A. Aguado,
1950, pp. 1113-16.
Sympathetic portrait of young BI. Stresses naturalness, vigor, spirit of
combat in BI's life and in his *La barraca*.

Bb154 Del Villar, Emilio H., '*Sangre y arena*', *Nuevo Mundo*, 750
(21.5.08).
On popularity of BI's works outside of Spain.

Bb155 Dendle, Brian J., 'BI and Coloma's *Pequeñeces*', *Romance
Notes*, VIII,2 (Spring 1967), 200-3.
How *La araña negra* refutes contentions of *Pequeñeces*.

Bb156 ——, 'The Racial Theories of Emilia Pardo Bazán', *Hispanic
Review*, XXXVIII,1 (1970), 17-31.
EPB's concept of racial heredity is more deterministic than are the
naturalistic theories of BI.

Bb157 ——, in *The Spanish Novel of Religious Thesis: 1876-1936*,
M: Princeton Univ.-Castalia, 1968, especially pp. 46-57.
Each of BI's works treating the religious question is carefully analysed
in this clear, illuminating study.

Bb158 Denjean, François, 'Un Écrivain espagnol ami de la France:
VBI et ses romans sur la guerre', *Athéna*, Paris, I,2 (1922),
119-30.
BI as a pro-French propagandist; examination of war novels.

Bb159 Deschamps, Gaston, 'Le Romancier BI', *Le Temps* (14.9.02).
Long subjective article on *La barraca*.

Bb160 Devlin, John, 'VBI', in *Spanish Anticlericalism: A Study in
Modern Alienation*, New York: Las Américas, 1966,
pp. 93-113.
Mainly on *El intruso, La catedral.* BI's republican anti-clericalism
becomes condemnation of religious spirit in general.

Bb161 Díaz del Moral, Juan, in *Historia de las agitaciones campe-
sinas andaluzas*, M: Alianza, 1967, p.186.
Notes BI's 1902 political excursions to Córdoba.

Bb162 Díaz-Pérez, Viriato, 'VBI', in Ac87. *

Bb163 Dicenta, Joaquín, '*La horda*', *EP* (10.7.05).
Compares novel with Baroja's *La busca*.

Bb164 Díez-Canedo, Enrique, '*Mare Nostrum*, novela de BI', in

Conversaciones literarias, M: Ed. América, 1921, pp. 121-31.
On novel's excessive length, weak protagonists.

Bb165 Domingo, José, 'BI: balance de un centenario', *Ínsula*, XXIII, 254 (Jan. 1968), 5-6.
Explains injustices of BI criticism.

Bb166 Domingo, Marcelino, 'La impresión de España: BI', *EP* (27.6.15).
Interview: BI laments Spain's indifference to France's fate in European War.

Bb167 Donoso, Ricardo, 'BI', *Atenea*, Santiago de Chile, V,1 (31.3.28), 26-9.
Praises author and his works.

Bb168 Dos Passos, John, 'An Inverted Midas', in *Rosinante to the Road Again*, New York: G.H. Doran, 1922, pp. 120-32.
About BI's 'popular vulgarization'. Despite fame in USA, BI will be only 'a seven days' marvel'.

Bb169 Dulzuras [pseud?], '*Sangre y arena*', *EP* (18.5.08).
Demonstrates accuracy of novel's taurine material.

Bb170 Durán y Tortajada, Enrique, 'BI, en Lo Rat Penat y en el Centro de Cultura Valenciana', *Las Provincias*, Val. (29.1.67).
Nature of BI's activities as a 'ratpenatista' and subsequent contact with the Centro.

Bb171 Edwards, Sarah S., 'BI,V. *Mexico in Revolution*, N.Y.: Dutton, 1920', *Southwestern Political Science Quarterly*, I,3 (1920), 304.
Excellent summation of contents and thesis of BI's book.

Bb172 Elías, Alfredo, 'Carta abierta a don VBI', *Hispania* (USA), IX,6 (1926), 341-4.
Ridicules BI as a person and author.

Bb173 Ellis, Havelock, 'BI', in *Views and Reviews*, Boston: Houghton-Mifflin, 1932, pp. 247-57. Reprint from *New Statesman* (30.5.14).
BI's work is losing the original fine quality of his regional novels.

Bb174 Entrambasaguas, Joaquín de, 'Bibliografía: VBI', in *Las mejores novelas españolas contemporáneas (1900-1904)*, vol. II, B: Planeta, 1958, pp. 1-80.
Essay on BI's life based largely on Gascó Contell's study with J.E.'s

disparaging comments on BI's character, politics. Finds only Valencian works to have literary value. Detailed analysis of *Entre naranjos*, text of which follows, pp. 81-338. Bibliography of some one hundred and fifty items has a number of errors.

Bb175 Eoff, Sherman H., 'VBI: *Cañas y barro* (1902)', in *The Modern Spanish Novel*, New York: New York Univ. Press, pp. 115-19.
Good study of the oneness of characters and nature in this novel.

Bb176 Ernest-Charles, J., 'BI', in *Les Samedis Littéraires*, vol. IV, Paris: E. Sansot, 1905, pp. 335-48. Also published as 'La Vie littéraire: BI', *Revue Bleue*, III,5 (1905), 663-6.
Explains BI's works to French readers.

Bb177 Erskine, Beatrice, 'VBI', *The Spectator*, London (4.2.28), 149-50.
Sympathetic review of BI's life; spirited interview with him.

Bb178 Escalante, Miguel Ángel, 'Notas sobre el estilo de VBI', *Cultura*, La Plata, II,8 (1950), 67-87.
Confused attempt to analyse BI's 'dynamic' and 'impatient' style.

Bb179 Escofet, José, 'Un *caso* en la literatura: la suerte de BI', *La Vanguardia* (18.10.24).
In Spain BI's works are widely read although their author is rarely mentioned; the opposite situation holds in France.

Bb180 Escola, Francisco, 'María Guerrero y BI', *Informaciones* (31.1.28).
Significance of their deaths for world of art.

Bb181 Espina, Antonio, 'Ojeada actualizante sobre BI', *Revista de Occidente*, XX,58 (Jan. 1968), 50-68.
Rambling essay full of digressions and factual errors; says almost nothing original or of value about BI.

Bb182 Estellés, José Luis, 'BI y *Mare Nostrum*', Val.: Prometeo, 1918, 30pp.
Reprint of a vapid eulogistic lecture.

Bb183 Estellés, Vicente Andrés, 'Puesta de sol en Fontana Rosa', *Las Provincias*, Val. (29.8.73).
BI's final years; autobiographical allusions in his works.

Bb184 Estévez Ortega, E., 'La última entrevista con BI', *Nuevo*

Mundo, XXXV,1777 (10.2.28).
Interesting wide-ranging interview.

Bb185 Eulalia, Infanta of Spain, in *Memoirs of a Spanish Princess*,
tr. by P. Mégrez, New York: W.W. Norton, 1937, p.222.
Spanish title: *Memorias de Doña Eulalia de Borbón*, B:
Ed. Juventud, 1934.
Enjoyed reading BI's novels but found him personally to be ungracious
and common.

Bb186 Fariña Núñez, Eloy, '*Sangre y arena*', *Nosotros*, B.A., III,
13-14 (1908), 109-13.
Introduction to novel.

Bb187 Farnell, Ida, 'VBI', in *Spanish Prose and Poetry*, Oxford:
Clarendon Press, 1920, pp. 163-8.
General comments on BI and his works; translates passage from *La
bodega*.

Bb188 Feldmann, Siegmund, 'BI en Alemania', *La República de
las Letras* (8.7.05).
Translation of Feldmann's newspaper article introducing BI to German
readers. See also Bb103.

Bb189 Fernández Almagro, Melchor, in *Historia política de la
España contemporánea 1897-1902*, M: Alianza, 1968,
pp. 281,283.
BI's fomenting of anti-clericalism.

Bb190 Fernández Cuenca, Carlos, 'La labor juvenil de BI', *La Época*
(31.8.29). More readily accessible in *Revista Americana de
Buenos Aires*, LXVII (1929), 305-8.
Informative account of some of BI's repudiated works.

Bb191 Fernández Flores, Wenceslao, 'BI', *EP* (7.2.28).
BI 'movía hacia España la simpatía universal'.

Bb192 ——, 'Comentarios: BI', *EP* (7.2.28).
BI's great kindness to other authors.

Bb193 Fernández Villegas, Francisco [pseud: Zeda], 'Alrededor de
Sangre y arena', *La Época* (4.6.08).
Praises author's psychological presentation of protagonist.

Bb194 ——, '*La bodega*, novela original de VBI', *La Época* (6.4.05).
Despite glaring weaknesses, it is one of BI's best novels.

Bb195 ——, 'Crónica literaria: *La barraca*', *La Época* (22.12.98).
On epic quality of novel and BI's power to touch readers' emotions.

Bb196 ——, 'Lecturas de la semana: *Cañas y barro*', *La Época* (19.1.03). Also in *La Lectura*, I (1903), 115-19.
BI is unequalled in descriptive powers and in communicating emotions.

Bb197 Ferrándiz Alborz, Francisco, 'Presencia de VBI', *Solidaridad Obrera*, Paris (Oct. 1961), 8-9. *

Bb198 Ferrer Roda, Julio, 'El ciclo valenciano en la novela de BI', *Reseña*, M, IV,20 (1967), 323-40.
On BI and Valencia; BI's error in abandoning Valencian theme; relationship of his stories and novels.

Bb199 Ferreras, Juan Ignacio, 'BI, V', in *La novela por entregas, 1840-1900*, M: Taurus, 1972, pp. 231-6.
Examines BI's early works *La araña negra, ¡Viva la República! , Los fanáticos*. Sheds light on these little-known works of political propaganda.

Bb200 ——, 'El *caso* BI', in *Tendencias de la novela española actual*, Paris: Ediciones Hispanoamericanas, 1970, pp. 30-1.
Penetrating observations on the problem of classifying BI as a novelist; BI's fundamental contribution to 20th-century Spanish novel.

Bb201 Ferreres, Rafael, 'Valencia y la novela del siglo XIX', *Feriario*, Val. (May 1947). *

Bb202 Fitzmaurice-Kelly, J., 'A Recent Spanish Novel', *The Athenaeum*, London, 4676 (12.12.19), 1351.
On BI's popularity and important works; *Los enemigos de la mujer*.

Bb203 Flynn, Gerard Cox, 'Yes, you do have Cervantes, but what else is there? ', *Hispania* (USA), XLIII,1 (1960), 74-7.
American prejudice against Hispanic literature stems partly from inadequate textbooks with their over-emphasis on *indianismo*, brave rebels, BI.

Bb204 Fontrodona, Mariano, 'BI', *Azor*, B, 26 (1967), 3.
BI's greatness is as a narrator and author of 'literatura imaginativa'.

Bb205 Forjaz de Sampaio, Albino, 'BI, su arte, su obra y su vida', *La Lectura*, I (1906), 223-4.
General introduction stressing BI's similarities to Zola. Reprinted from *O Século*, Lisbon.

Bb206 Fox, Edward Inman, in *Azorín as a Literary Critic*, New York:

Hispanic Institute, 1962, p.23.
Young Martínez Ruiz contributed to BI's *El Pueblo.*

Bb207 Francés, José, 'BI o el genio novelesco', in *De la condición del escritor: algunos ejemplos*, M: Paez-Bolsa, 1930, pp. 25-55.
Various anecdotes and observations about BI's character.

Bb208 ——, '*La bodega*, por VBI', *La Lectura*, I (1905), 436-40.
Excellent analysis of novel.

Bb209 ——, 'El gran español, novelista del mundo', *Nuevo Mundo* (3.2.28).
On themes and characters of BI's works.

Bb210 ——, '*La horda*, por VBI', *La Lectura*, II (1905), 277-80.
On plot, themes, relationship to Baroja's novels.

Bb211 ——, '*La maja desnuda*, por VBI', *La Lectura*, II (1906), 195-9.
Defends work against hostile critics; unlike BI's previous political novels, this is a triumph of art.

Bb212 ——, 'El poderoso visionario', *EP* (29.10.33).
Few Spanish authors equalled BI as a great visionary.

Bb213 ——, 'Una novela de BI', *Nuevo Mundo* (19.5.16).
Enthusiastic appraisal of BI's *Historia de la guerra europea* and *Los cuatro jinetes del Apocalipsis*; attacks Spain's indifference to the war.

Bb214 Francos Rodríguez, J., 'El libro del día: *La bodega*', *El Heraldo de Madrid* (2.3.05). *

Bb215 Fundenburg, George B., and John F. Klein, introduction to *El préstamo de la difunta*, New York: Century, 1925, pp.v-vii.
Concise, accurate sketch of BI's life and works.

Bb216 Fuster, Joan, 'Los excéntricos del 98', *Levante*, Val. (1.10.60).
Excellent article on what unites BI with and what separates him from authors of generation of 1898.

Bb217 ——, 'Recuerdo y juicio de BI en su centenario', *Destino*, B, 1540 (11.2.67), 16-19.
Blasquismo on regional and national level; BI's attitude towards *valencianismo* and Valencian *Renaixença*.

Bb218 ——, 'Recuerdo y juicio de BI en su centenario – Don Vicente,

hombre de acción', *Destino*, B, 1542 (25.2.67), 32-5.
The many sides of BI: politician, adventurer, writer, publisher, millionaire. Attempts to define BI as a politician but to show his poverty of ideas as an ideologue.

Bb219 —, 'Recuerdo y juicio de BI en su centenario – su obra literaria', *Destino*, B, 1541 (18.2.67), 32-7.
Theorizes on causes of Spanish critics' scorn of BI's works. Observations on selected novels and literary influences on BI.

Bb220 García Sanchiz, Federico, 'VBI', in *Tierras, tiempos y vida: memorias*, vol. I, M: Ed. Biosca, 1959, pp. 149-61.
Condescending and impressionistic observations on BI's character. Covers period of more than twenty years but lacks temporal framework.

Bb221 Gascó Contell, Emilio, 'Las cuatro vidas de VBI', *Levante*, Val. (27.1.61).
In activity and accomplishment the four periods of BI's life equal four separate lives.

Bb222 —, introduction to *Discursos literarios*, Ac127, pp. 7-33.
Eulogistic introduction to reprint of BI's speeches is largely composed of quotations from BI himself.

Bb223 —, 'En el aniversario: algunas novelas póstumas de BI', *Gaceta Literaria*, IV,76 (15.2.30), p.5.
BI's declining health from 1916 onwards; details on *La voluntad de vivir, El águila y la serpiente, La juventud del mundo*, BI's unpublished works.

Bb224 —, 'Polifacético BI', *La Estafeta Literaria*, 363 (1967), 11-12.
BI's life divided into periods around certain highpoints.

Bb225 —, 'Quelques oeuvres posthumes de VBI', *Revue de l'Amérique Latine*, Paris, XV,75 (1928), 239-43.
Comments on never-published *El águila y la serpiente*; also on final novels, plans prior to death.

Bb226 —, 'Sobre la aventura argentina de VBI', *Libros Selectos*, México, 16 (1963). *

Bb227 Gascón, Antonio, 'BI y el cine', *La Pantalla*, 6 (3.2.28), 83.
On BI's keen understanding of cinematography; list of some of his novels that were filmed.

Bb228 Gazul, Arturo, 'Recuerdo de una visita a BI', *EP* (1.3.28).
BI disclaimed involvement in abortive armed uprising against Spanish dictatorship.

Bb229 Gerli, E. Michael, 'BI's *Flor de Mayo*, Sorolla, and Impressionism', *Iberoromania*, new series, I,1 (1974), pp. 121-9.
Suggestive exploration of relationship between BI and the impressionist painter Sorolla; examines influence of pictorial art on BI's Valencian novels.

Bb230 Gil Casado, Pablo, in *La novela social española (1942-1968)*, B: Seix Barral, 1968, pp. xxxi-xxxii.
On BI as a precursor of the social novel.

Bb231 Glascock, Clyde Chew, 'VBI and his Work', *Texas Review*, VI (1921), 267-91, and VII (1921), 17-35.
Progresses chronologically through BI's novels summarizing plot and commenting on various aspects of each one. Introductory study intended for readers who know no Spanish.

Bb232 Goemare, P., 'BI, pamphlétaire', *Revue Belge*, Bruxelles, II,1 (1925). *

Bb233 Goldberg, Isaac, 'BI: The Man and his Work', *Stratford Journal*, Boston, IV (1919), 235-44.
Despite its excessive praise, Goldberg's survey has perceptive observations on BI's popularity and works.

Bb234 ——, 'VBI', *The Dial*, LXV,777 (1918), 415-17.
BI's strengths and weaknesses as a novelist; discussion of war novels.

Bb235 Gómez Carrillo, Enrique, 'París: el gaucho BI', *El Liberal* (29.10.09).
On BI in the Chaco.

Bb236 Gómez de Baquero, Eduardo [pseud: Andrenio], '*Argentina y sus grandezas*, por VBI', *Los Lunes de 'El Imparcial'* (18.8.10).
Analyses genre and describes circumstances of new book.

Bb237 ——, 'BI', in *El renacimiento de la novela española en el siglo XIX*, M: Mundo Latino, 1924, pp. 96-101.
Concise sketch of man and his works.

Bb238 ——, '*Cañas y barro*: La filosofía de Sangonera', *La España Moderna*, XV,170 (1903), 172-8.
Why this is one of the finest of modern Spanish novels; echoes of Tolstoy in character Sangonera.

Bb239 —— , 'El caso de BI', in *De Gallardo a Unamuno*, M:

Espasa-Calpe, 1926, pp. 249-66.
On Spanish hostility towards BI; review of his writings; good analysis of *La reina Calafia.*

Bb240 —— , '*La catedral*', *La España Moderna*, XV,180 (1903), 154-61. Also in *Letras e ideas*, B: Henrich y Cía, 1905 pp. 138-47.
Unfavorable review; examines possible literary antecedents for novel.

Bb241 —— , '*La horda*, novela por VBI', *La España Moderna*, XVII,3 (1905), 163-72.
Sensitive analysis of BI's description of social milieu, social philosophy in *La horda.*

Bb242 —— , '*Luna Benamor*, novela por VBI', *Los Lunes de 'El Imparcial'* (7.6.09).
Detailed review of novel.

Bb243 —— , '*La maja desnuda*, novela por VBI', *La España Moderna*, XVIII,3 (1906), 175-82.
Stresses convincing psychological presentation of artist Renovales.

Bb244 —— , 'Muerte de un gran novelista', *El Sol* (29.1.28).
Sensitive essay on life and works of BI. Regrets never having written a book about deceased friend's writings.

Bb245 —— , '*Los muertos mandan*, novela por VBI', *La España Moderna*, XXI,244 (1909), 162-8.
On philosophical, mythical, and descriptive elements of novel.

Bb246 —— , 'Novelistas españoles modernos. Las novelas de BI', *Cultura Española*, IV,12 (1908), 937-51.
General characterization of BI's writing with a clearly drawn survey of his novels.

Bb247 —— . '*Oriente*, por VBI', *Los Lunes de 'El Imparcial'* (27.1.08).
One of the few detailed reviews of this travel book.

Bb248 —— , '*Sangre y arena*, de BI, y *El espada*, de Héctor Abreu', *El Imparcial* (25.6.08).
Documented refutation of Dr Pardales's charge of plagiarism against BI (see Ba71).

Bb249 —— , '*Sangre y arena*, novela de BI', *El Imparcial* (6.5.08).
Highly favorable review of novel.

Bb250 —— , 'Un embajador de las letras españolas en América', *El*

Imparcial (10.3.09).
Why BI is the best ambassador for Spanish letters in Spanish America.

Bb251 —, 'Zola en España', *La Gaceta Literaria*, I,21 (1.11.27).
Arroz y tartana is BI's most Zolaesque work; his Valencian masterpieces have no trace of Zola. The city novels reflect slightly the plan of *Les Trois Villes*.

Bb252 Gómez de la Serna, Ramón, 'VBI', in *Nuevos retratos contemporáneos*, B.A.: Ed. Sudamericana, 1945, pp. 129-37.
Biographical highlights; anecdotes; meetings with BI.

Bb253 Gómez Molleda, María Dolores, in *Los reformadores de la España contemporánea*, M: Consejo Superior de Investigaciones Científicas, 1966, p.430.
Cites claim of rightist press that BI, Canalejas, Romero Robledo exploited anti-clericalism for financial gain.

Bb254 González-Blanco, Andrés, in *Historia de la novela en España desde el romanticismo a nuestros días*, M: Sáenz de Jubera, 1909, pp. 588-93; 636-47.
Mostly subjective and pedantic comments on Valencian novels and *La horda*.

Bb255 González Fiol, Enrique, 'VBI, novelista . . . o lo que sea', in *Domadores del éxito: confesiones de su vida y de su obra*, M: Sociedad Editorial de España, n.d., pp. 120-63.
On the dichotomy in BI's character; interview covering BI's lifelong political and literary activities.

Bb256 González Martí, Manuel, 'Emilia Pardo Bazán y BI', *Levante*, Val. (5.2.61).
BI as EPB's guide during her Valencian visit; how each signed the other's short story later submitted to a literary competition.

Bb257 —, 'Mi admiración por BI', *Las Provincias*, Val. (29.1.67).
The nonagenarian MGM provides valuable information on youthful BI; the relationship of the two men.

Bb258 —, 'Las salas personales del Museo Nacional de Cerámica: la del novelista BI', *Levante: Suplemento Gráfico de los Domingos*, Val. (29.1.67).
Contents of BI room in the Museum; illustrated.

Bb259 González-Ruano, César, 'Las dedicatorias de Valle-Inclán a BI son auténticas', *EP* (18.2.28).
Attempts to prove that Valle-Inclán, despite denials, dedicated copies

of *Las sonatas* to BI.

Bb260 ——, 'VBI', in *Siluetas de escritores contemporáneos*, M: Ed. Nacional, 1949, pp. 73-5.
Found BI a pitiable figure during chance meeting in Paris.

Bb261 González Ruiz, Nicolás, 'VBI', in *En esta hora, ojeada a los valores literarios*, M: Talleres Voluntad, 1925, pp.169-76.
Criticizes BI's naturalism and anticlericalism.

Bb262 Gracia Azorín, Abel, 'Mi maestro VBI', *EP* (4.3.28).
BI's secretary recalls his last year of life.

Bb263 Gramberg, Eduard J., 'Tres tipos de ambientación en la novela del siglo diecinueve', *Revista Hispánica Moderna*, XXVIII,2-4 (1962), 315-26.
Excellent study. Contrasts function of setting in novels by Pereda, Clarín, and BI.

Bb264 Granjel, Luis S., in *La generación literaria del noventa y ocho*, Salamanca: Anaya, 1966, pp. 73; 81; 109-11; 228; 233-4.
Mostly on BI's connections with youthful turn-of-century literary and journalistic groups.

Bb265 —— , in *Panorama de la generación del 98*, M: Guadarrama, 1959, p.19.
BI against political-literary perspective of '98.

Bb266 Guerlin, Henri, in *L'Espagne moderne vue par ses écrivains*, Paris: Perrin, 1924, pp. 65-6; 161-91.
Plot summary with some analysis of *Sangre y arena* and four Valencian novels.

Bb267 Hernández-Girbal, F., in *Una vida pintoresca: Manuel Fernández y González*, M: Biblioteca Atlántico, 1931, pp. 277-87.
Best account of BI's youthful collaboration with MFG.

Bb268 Hespelt, E. Herman, 'Source or Analogue of BI's "El golpe doble"? ', *Spanish Review* (New York), no.1 (1934), 68-9.
On similarity of story in English traveller's account of Spain to 'El golpe doble'.

Bb269 Hind, Charles Lewis, 'VBI', in *More Authors and I*, New York: Dodd, Mead, 1922, pp. 165-9.
Clever advertising was responsible for popularity of BI's works in America. On BI's skills as public lecturer.

Bb270 Hispanic Society of America, staff members of, in
A History of the Hispanic Society of America 1904-54,
New York, 1954, pp. 52; 343; 350; 548; 557.
BI's visit, lectures in New York; his portrait, life mask, other items held
by HSA.

Bb271 Howells, William Dean, 'Editor's Easy Chair', *Harper's
Monthly Magazine*, CXXXI,786 (1915), 957-60.
Overly enthusiastic and uncritical praise for BI's fiction; discussion of
Sangre y arena and *La catedral.*

Bb272 ——, in BI's *The Shadow of the Cathedral*, tr. Mrs W.A. Gillespie, New York: Dutton, 1919 reprint, pp. v-xix.
Introduction to BI and *La catedral*; judges BI to be the finest of Spanish
novelists living outside of Spain, and Spanish novelists to be the best in
Europe.

Bb273 Hughes, H.B.L., 'BI and the Catholic Church', *The Catholic
World*, CXX,719 (1925), 604-8.
Origins of BI's hostility towards Catholicism; *La catedral* reveals BI's
ignorance of Catholic theology.

Bb274 Ibáñez Rizo, Ernesto, 'BI, abogado', *EP* (29.10.33).
Rare account of BI's brief career as a lawyer.

Bb275 Iden, Otto, 'Der spanische Romanschriftsteller VBI', *Zeit-
schrift für Neusprachlichen Unterricht*, XXII (1923), 110-21.
Synthesis of life; comments mostly on anti-German war novels.

Bb276 Iglesias Hermida, Prudencio, in *Hombres y cosas de mi patria
y de mi tiempo*, M: Sáez Hermanos, 1914, pp. 42-5.
BI's physiognomy; his descriptive skills and artistic decline.

Bb277 ——, 'VBI', in *De mi museo*, M: Imprenta Ibérica, 1909,
pp. 37-46.
Repeats part of Bb276, but adds unflattering characterization of *levantinos* in general.

Bb278 Ingram, Rex, 'Mi amigo BI', *EP* (29.10.33).
Anecdotes; BI's ideas on motion pictures; his dream of a Mediterranean
cultural union.

Bb279 Insúa, Alberto, 'Estimación de BI', *La Prensa*, B.A. (5.3.39).
Positive and negative features of BI's style.

Bb280 ——, 'Mi amistad con el maestro', *EP* (29.10.33).
Various meetings with BI.

Bb281 —, 'Sobre *La horda*', *El País* (27.6.05).

Important study: on Baroja's possible influence on BI, *La horda*'s sexually daring passages, etc.

Bb282 —, 'Un español universal: BI', *Atenea*, Santiago de Chile (31.3.28), 30-4.

How World War made BI an international author; BI's disregard for stylistic niceties.

Bb283 Iris [pseud.], 'BI: impresiones', *El Mercurio*, Santiago-Valparaíso (29.11.09).

Despite prejudice against BI for his anti-Catholicism, his lecture enchanted her and audience. Feels a new sympathy for BI's personality and works.

Bb284 Jaén, Ramón, 'Spanish Fiction in the United States', *The Nation*, New York, CVI,2749 (1918), 261.

Spanish literature is finally becoming known in USA through translations of Galdós and BI. Uniqueness of Spanish regions requires good introduction to each of their novels for the American reader.

Bb285 Jaloux, Edmond, 'L'Esprit des livres: VBI', *Les Nouvelles Littéraires* (4.2.28).

Evokes BI, his love for France.

Bb286 Jerique, José, 'BI nos dice . . . ', *La Nación*, B.A. (19.2.28).

Interview: mainly on literary rights of recent novels in USA.

Bb287 Jover, José María, 'De la literatura a la historia: La Valencia de la restauración en la retina de BI', *Hispania*, M, XXVI,104 (1966), 599-605.

Enthusiastic review of E. Sebastià's study on BI: Ba89.

Bb288 Juderías, Julián, '*Novelistas españoles contemporáneos, VBI*, por L. Schepelevich', *La Lectura*, III (1905), 347-9.

A review-article on a Russian book which, despite Juderías' title, was on a number of novelists and was not in Spanish.

Bb289 Juliá Martínez, Eduardo, 'Una obra de BI olvidada', *El Libro Español*, II,17 (May 1959), 298-304.

Mostly on *Caerse del cielo* and its connection with BI's other works.

Bb290 Just, Juli, 'Joaquín Sorolla et BI', *La Dépêche du Midi*, Toulouse (28.8.62).

Similarities between painter and author; parallels in their careers and their works.

Bb291 ——, 'VBI', *España Libre*, New York (Nov.-Dec., 1967), 6.
On BI's life-long struggle for a Spanish republic.

Bb292 Kaufman, Eugenia, 'VBI: *La reina Calafia*', *Books Abroad*, I,3 (1927), 93.
Brief summary and commentary on novel.

Bb293 Keniston, Hayward, 'An Apostle of New Spain', *The Nation*, New York, LXXXVII,2269 (1908), 622-3.
BI promulgates a movement for national regeneration. Good appraisal of life and works.

Bb294 ——, 'Ibáñez', *The New Republic*, XX,260 (1919), 12-14.
Reviews six novels translated into English.

Bb295 Keniston, Hayward, and L.B. Kiddle, eds., *La barraca*, New York: Holt, Rinehart, 1960, pp. ix-xvii.
Concise, factual introduction to BI and *La barraca*.

Bb296 Kercheville, F.M., and R. Hale, 'Ibáñez and Spanish Republic-anism', *Modern Language Journal*, XVII,5 (1933), 342-8.
Superficially compares political and religious views developed in BI's novels to those expounded by the Spanish Republic.

Kiddle, L.B.: see Keniston, H.

Bb297 King, Georgiana G., 'Ibáñez, Huysmans, and George Meredith', *The Bookman*, New York, XLIX (March, 1919), 71-2.
Finds BI's *La catedral* superior to Huysmans's novel of same title, and reminiscent of certain passages of Meredith.

Bb298 ——, 'Translating more Ibáñez', *The Bookman*, New York, XLIX (May, 1919), 345-7.
English translations of BI's works are often defective.

Klein, J.F.: see Fundenburg, G.B.

Bb299 Leavitt, Sturgis E., in *Siete cuentos de VBI*, New York: H. Holt, 1926, pp.i-xiv.
Leavitt's introduction on BI's life, popularity, works, precedes six stories gathered together from three collections.

Bb300 LeGentil, Georges, '*La Cathédrale*, de M. BI', *La Revue Latine*, IV (25.6.05).
Review stresses author's attack on Spanish traditions, analysis of character G. Luna, esthetic treatment of Toledo cathedral.

Bb301 León, Ricardo, 'Impresiones de un libro: *La catedral*', *EP*

(12.12.03).
Symbolism in the novel; contrast with certain French novels.

Bb302 León Roca, J.L., 'El alma valenciana de BI', *Las Provincias*, Val. (29.1.67).
Valencia in the life, spirit and works of BI.

Bb303 ——, 'Los años heroicos de VBI', *Universidad*, Santa Fe (Arg.), 47 (Jan.-March, 1961), 49-65.
On BI's political activities 1890-1906 in Valencia.

Bb304 ——, 'Cómo escribió BI *La barraca*', *Les Langues Néo-Latines*, 180 (April, 1967), 1-22.
Information from *EP* on BI's early works. Amplifies BI's own statements on expansion of his short story into novel *La barraca*.

Bb305 ——, in *Crónicas de viaje*, Ac128, pp. 7-23.
León Roca provides introductory comments in his prologue to edition of BI's travel sketches.

Bb306 ——, 'Fuentes de inspiración de dos cuentos de VBI', *Universidad*, Santa Fe (Arg.), 45 (July-Sept., 1960), 151-7.
BI's prison experiences inspired 'La condenada' and 'Un funcionario'.

Bb307 ——, 'La obra periodística de BI', *Levante: Suplemento Gráfico de los Domingos*, Val. (29.1.67).
The different stages in BI's journalistic career.

Bb308 ——, 'Un cuento no coleccionado de BI', *Les Langues Néo-Latines*, 180 (April, 1967), 23-30.
Reprints forgotten '¡Mátala!' from *El Imparcial.* See Ac53.

Bb309 Lerroux, Alejandro, 'BI', *La Publicidad* (26.9.03).
Long laudatory article. Exhorts Barcelona Republicans to receive BI warmly.

Bb310 Levi, Ezio, 'BI', in *Nella letteratura spagnola contemporanea (Saggi)*, Firenze: La Voce, 1922, pp. 13-36.
On BI's dramatic life; refutes Pitollet's denial that Freya in BI's *Mare Nostrum* is based partly on spy Mata Hari (see Bb436).

Bb311 Lorente, Juan José, '*El intruso*', *EP* (2.7.04).
Novel closely reflects Spanish reality; it effectively combats Jesuits.

Bb312 Loubès, Jean-Noël, 'Le Thème de la mort dans l'oeuvre romanesque de VBI', in *Pensée ibérique et finitude*, Univ. de Toulouse-Le Mirail, Série A, XVII (1972), pp. 59-76.
Death theme in selected works: its significance, possible sources, parallel

use in other authors.

Bb313 Luna, Dr Joaquín de, 'BI', *EP* (9.2.28).
BI's final comments on his health. Why he resembled Balzac more than Zola.

Bb314 ——, 'Unamuno y BI en París', *La Nación*, B.A. (27.8.33).
BI outshone Unamuno as a speaker; their difficult relationship; BI's *gaffes* in French.

Bb315 Lundeberg, Olav K., 'The Sand-Chopin Episode in *Los muertos mandan*', *Hispania* (USA), XV,2 (1932), 135-40.
BI carelessly distorts facts concerning this interpolated episode.

Bb316 Llombart, Constantí, in *Los fills de la morta-viva (apunts bio-bibliogràfichs)*, Val.: Ed. Emili Pasqual, 1879 [1883], p.765.
Cites BI as author of historical legends in *llemosí* and winner of 'accésit' in 1883 Jochs Florals.

Bb317 Llorente, Teodoro, 'El movimiento literario en Valencia en 1888', *La España Moderna*, I,1 (1889), 151-60.
Young BI follows tradition of V. Boix and F. Pizcueta. Positive judgments of five early works. Predicts BI will eventually write outstanding novels.

Bb318 ——, 'VBI: *Oriente*', *Cultura Española*, X,2 (1908), 414-6.
Thoughtful review and analysis.

Bb319 M.A., 'Hablando con BI', *El Diluvio* (15.6.16).
Barcelona interview on the War and writing of *Mare Nostrum*.

Bb320 Machado, Manuel, '¡Cuánta gente!', in Ba27, p.164.
Very brief poem to BI.

Bb321 Maeztu, Ramiro de, 'Apuntes para un manual sobre el vigente Katipunan literario', *Las Noticias*, B (14.12.1900). *
Satirizes K, imaginary Madrid society that promotes its authors and also has branches in provinces (VBI, Clarín).

Bb322 ——, 'BI', in *Las letras y la vida en la España de entreguerra*, M: Ed. Nacional, 1958, pp. 200-4. From *El Pueblo Vasco*, Bilbao (21.4.32).
Maeztu supports those who claim BI became a believer in Catholicism shortly before he died.

Bb323 Maicas, Víctor, 'BI y Azorín', *Senyera*, México (1.11.72).
Contrasts literary style of two authors.

Bb324 ——, 'La novelística de BI', *Las Provincias*, Val. (29.1.67).
Principal features of BI's personality and novels.

Bb325 Malboysson, Enrique, 'BI y Primo de Rivera', *EP* (18.3.30).
Comparison of the two Spaniards.

Bb326 Manchester, Paul T., ed., *La barraca*, New York: Macmillan, 1933, pp. vii-xvii.
Introduction to BI's life and writings.

Bb327 Maqueda, José, 'BI e a sua obra', *Gazeta Literária*, Porto, V,57 (1957), p.80.
General survey of BI's works.

Bb328 Marañón, Gregorio, in *Ensayo biológico sobre Enrique IV de Castilla y su tiempo*, M: Espasa-Calpe, 1941, p.118.
BI makes 'una apología partidista e inadmisible de Don Enrique' in his *En busca del Gran Kan.*

Bb329 Marçà, R., 'Taula redona sobre BI', *Gorg*, Val., III,17 (1971), 24-7.
Differing views on BI's politics by A. Cucó, J.L. León Roca, J. Marqués, R. Ninyoles.

Bb330 Marquina, Eduardo, 'VBI', in Ba27, pp. 159-61.
Long poem dedicated to BI's full life.

Bb331 Martínez, Graciano, 'La última novela de BI', in *De paso por las bellas letras*, vol. I, M: Eds Hispano-americanas, 1921, pp. 83-99.
Father Martínez's unfavorable review of *El intruso*; how its message ruins its artistry.

Bb332 Martínez de la Riva, Ramón, 'El hombre del baúl de la literatura española', *Blanco y Negro*, XXIV,1722 (1924).
BI's fame and travels make him the ambassador of Spanish letters throughout the world.

Bb333 Martínez Ruiz, José [pseud: Azorín], 'La amada España: Valencia', *La Vanguardia* (13.5.17).
Evokes university days and figure of BI.

Bb334 ——, 'BI', in *Valencia, OC*, vol. VI, M: Aguilar, 1948, pp. 95-7.
Portrait of BI; his literary style, its weaknesses and strengths.

Bb335 ——, 'BI en su reclinatorio', in *Varios hombres y algunas mujeres*, B: Ed. Aedos, 1962, pp. 211-16.
Sketch of BI writing *El Papa del mar.*

Bb336 ——, 'El campo del arte', in *Escritores*, M: Biblioteca Nueva, 1956, pp. 219-25. Reprinted from *ABC* (26.7.24).
Observations on *Novelas de la Costa Azul* and how literary tastes change.

Bb337 ——, 'Los dos mundos', in *Los Quintero y otras páginas*, *OC*, vol. IV, M: Aguilar, 1948, pp. 715-22.
Azorín retells story of *La reina Calafia* and comments on BI.

Bb338 ——, 'Francia: deplorable diplomacia', *ABC* (19.2.15).
Strongly attacks BI's Sorbonne speech linking support for Germany to certain political groups in Spain.

Bb339 ——, '*La horda*, última novela de BI', *EP* (16.7.05). Reprinted from *El Pueblo de Alicante*.
Detailed favorable review.

Bb340 ——, 'Nuestra réplica', *ABC* (9.3.15).
Replies to BI's letter in *El País* (8.3.15) regarding Azorín's previous criticism of BI's Sorbonne speech by reiterating his criticism of introducing political controversy into a literary gathering.

Bb341 Mata, Pedro, 'Crónica: la regeneración de Maltrana', *EP* (11.8.05).
Imagined encounter with protagonist of *La horda*.

Bb342 Maurevert, Georges, 'BI cuenta su viaje alrededor del mundo', *La Nación*, B.A. (1.6.24).
Interview; interesting anecdotes.

Bb343 Maury, Lucien, 'VBI: *En la sombra de La catedral*', *La España Moderna*, XIX,227 (1907), 95-102. Tr. of article appearing first in the *Revue Bleue*, unknown date.
Compares BI's *La catedral* to works by Hugo and Huysmans; novel's strong and weak points.

Bb344 Meliá, J.A., 'Bibliografía: *La maja desnuda*', *Revista Socialista*, 86 (1906), 447-8.
Stresses novel's skillfully drawn characters.

Bb345 Meliá Bernabeu, José María [pseud: Pigmalión], 'BI, Costa y la cultura popular', *El Liberal* (27.10.33).
BI's concern for mass education; invites Joaquín Costa to inaugurate his Universidad Popular.

Bb346 ——, 'BI en Provenza', *La Semana Literaria*, 63 (5.11.38), 6-8. Same article reprinted as 'BI y *Los cuatro jinetes del Apocalip-*

sis', *Levante*, Val. (5.6.66).
About BI's model for protagonist Desnoyers in *Los cuatro jinetes del Apocalipsis.*

Bb347 ——, 'Mi amistad con BI', in Ba59, pp. 75-90.
Recalls how as a boy he met BI; describes typical activity at BI's home.

Bb348 Melián Lafinur, Álvaro, 'BI', in *Temas hispánicos*, B.A.: Institución Cultural Española, 1943, pp. 175-87.
Repeats many commonplaces about BI.

Bb349 Mencken, H.L., in 'Introduction' to Pío Baroja's *Youth and Egolatry*, tr. by J.S. Fassett and F.L. Phillips, New York: Knopf, 1920, pp. 16-20.
In comparing BI with Baroja, Mencken finds BI to be a man of 'feeble intrinsic merits . . . half charlatan . . . less Spanish than French'.

Bb350 Menéndez Pidal, Ramón, in Ba27, p.77.
Judges BI's historical novels to be a praiseworthy patriotic achievement. Mentions frequent correspondence with BI.

Bb351 Mérimée, E., 'BI et le roman de moeurs provinciales', *Bulletin Hispanique*, V (1903), 272-300.
Contrasts the provincial and the urban novel; then analyses BI's Valencian works.

Bb352 Mérimée, Henri, 'Le Romancier BI et la cité de Valence', *Bulletin Hispanique*, XXIV (1922), 361-77.
Key events in BI's life; his expanding horizons; Valencia in his works.

Bb353 Merry del Val, Marquis de, 'The *Decadence* of Modern Spain', *The Sphere*, London, CX,1443 (1927), 446.
Spanish ambassador to Court of St James answers BI's attack on military dictatorship as published by V.J. Bordeux, Bb88.

Bb354 Mesa y Rosales, Enrique de, in *Tragicomedia*, M: Biblioteca Mignon, 1910, pp. 82-3. *
'Plumitas' episode in *Sangre y arena* is based on newspaper accounts of the bandit Pernales.

Bb355 Milego, Julio, 'BI y Valencia', *EP* (15.6.15).
Plea for BI to return to politics.

Bb356 ——, 'El mundo político: BI y Valencia', *EP* (15.6.15).
On rumors of BI's plans for renewed political action. How his return would resuscitate Republicanism in Valencia.

Bb357 Millas Covas, Jaime M., 'VBI, periodista y político', *Triunfo*,

571 (8.9.73), 30-5.
BI's achievement as journalist in Valencia, Madrid, abroad; examines his political role on the Valencian and national scenes.

Bb358 Miralles, Valerià, *'El valencianisme polític*, de la tertulia a l'*underground'*, *Gorg*, Val., 20 (1971), 26-9.
Review of A. Cucó's book and its section on BI (Bb148).

Bb359 Modave, Jeanine, 'BI et le naturalisme français', *Les Lettres Romanes*, XII (1958), 287-301.
In *Sónnica* BI plagiarizes Flaubert and P. Louÿs.

Bb360 Mogort Solanes, Felipe, 'BI, colonizador', *Caras y Caretas*, B.A., 2081 (20.8.38), pp. 111-15; 120.
Chronicle of BI's colonizing efforts in Argentina; eventual success of Nueva Valencia.

Bb361 Molina, Antonio F., 'VBI', in *La generación del 98*, B: Labor, 1968, p.68.
Characterizes BI as a second-rate author.

Bb362 Molina, Rodrigo A., *'BI, Unamuno, Valle-Inclán, Baroja: Cuatro individualistas de España'*, in *Estudios*, M: Ínsula, 1961, pp. 121-3.
Review of J.A. Balseiro's book (Ba5).

Bb363 Momblanch y Gonzálbez, Francisco de P., in *Historia de la Albufera de Valencia*, Val.: Publicaciones del Archivo Municipal, 1960, pp. 31-2.
Background for BI's 'Sancha' legend in *Cañas y barro*.

Bb364 Monguió, Luis, 'Crematística de los novelistas españoles del siglo XIX', *Revista Hispánica Moderna*, XVII (1951), 111-27.
Excellent study on literary earnings of BI and other novelists.

Bb365 Monte-Cristo, M., 'Una comida en honor de BI', *El Imparcial* (4.6.21).
Detailed account of event, important guests, etc.

Bb366 Montero, Alonso José, 'El republicano que no vio la República', *Nuevo Mundo* (14.4.32).
BI's voice is missed now that his beloved Republic has been proclaimed.

Bb367 Morby, Edwin S., 'William Dean Howells and Spain', *Hispanic Review*, XIV,3 (1946), 187-212.
On Howells's excessive enthusiasm for and misunderstanding of certain Spanish realist novelists, including BI.

Bb368 Mori, Arturo, 'La gesta revolucionaria: BI vuelve a España', *El Liberal* (29.10.33).
On reburial of BI's remains in a Republican Spain.

Bb369 Morote, Luis, 'Artista revolucionario', *EP* (12.3.04).
On how *La catedral* has scandalized Spanish reactionaries.

Bb370 ——, 'Autores y libros: *Sangre y arena*', *El Heraldo de Madrid* (8.5.08).
Praises novel for its penetrating social, psychological analysis.

Bb371 ——, '*Cañas y barro*', *El Heraldo de Madrid* (15.1.03).
Excellent, balanced review of novel; finds it superior to *La barraca*.

Bb372 ——, '*La catedral*, novela de BI', in *Pasados por agua*, Val.: Sempere, 1904, pp. 183-98. Reprinted from *El Heraldo de Madrid* (8.11.03).
Perceptive analysis of the novel.

Bb373 ——, '*La horda*', in *Teatro y novela: artículos críticos 1903-1906*, M: Fernando Fe, 1906, pp. 223-35. From *El Heraldo de Madrid* (23.6.05).
Stresses social, esthetic values of novel.

Bb374 ——, '*El intruso*', *EP* (19.6.04).
Examines novel's thesis, characters, consequences.

Bb375 ——, 'El libro del día', *EP* (20.5.06).
Morote's impressions on reading *La maja desnuda*.

Bb376 ——, 'Literatura valenciana', *El Liberal* (30.7.96).
Examines BI's *Flor de Mayo* and works by Ismael Rizo and Dr Cervera Barat.

Bb377 Moses, Montrose J., 'BI the Approachable', *New York Times*, sect. 9 (2.11.19).
BI aboard ship and on arrival in New York. His human warmth, popularity, ideas on America and its literature, etc.

B378 Moulin, René, 'Una entrevista con el gran escritor BI', *EP* (26.2.15).
BI's comments on Spanish Germanophiles and the allied cause.

B379 Moutet, Marius, 'La Francia judicial y BI', *EP* (29.10.33).
Given France's gratitude to BI, no French court could have found him guilty of charges brought by a Spanish Germanophile king.

B380 Murga, Alfredo, '*Cañas y barro*: novela de VBI', *El Liberal* (1.4.03).
Prize-winning critical essay on novel in competition held by *El Liberal*.

Bb381 Navarro Ledesma, F. [abbr: FNL], 'Bibliografía: *El intruso*, novela por BI', *ABC* (7.7.04).
As with *Electra*, the social or political impact matters more than its literary value.

Bb382 ——, 'Gacetilla literaria: *La horda*, por VBI', *ABC* (25.6.05).
Considers it one of finest Spanish descriptive novels although marred by justifiable social propaganda.

Bb383 —— [abbr: N], 'El libro de la semana', *ABC* (1.1.03).
Reviews *Cañas y barro*; BI's finest novel, a work of 'grandiosidad tolstoiana'.

Bb384 Nazary, 'La canción del domingo', *EP* (10.5.08).
Imagery of *Sangre y arena* compensates for stylistic defects mentioned by critics. Language of novel is not offensive, for many euphemisms replace cruder terms of the *corrida*.

Bb385 Ninyoles, Rafael Lluis, 'Literatura o literatures?', *Serra d'Or*, B (June 1968), 79-80.
Traces linguistic conflict in Valencia as background for language in which BI, C. Llombart, T. Llorente, etc., each chose to write.

Bb386 *Nosotros*, la dirección de, 'La demostración de *Nosotros* a BI', *Nosotros*, B.A., IV,22-3 (1909), 366-71.
Details of banquet honoring BI.

Bb387 Nuez, Sebastián de la, and José Schraibman, eds, *Cartas del archivo de Pérez Galdós*, M: Taurus, 1967, pp. 125-6.
Introductory notes to 'Cartas de BI'. See also Ad8.

Bb388 Ombuena, José, 'Los muertos mandan', *Las Provincias*, Val. (29.1.67).
Editor of daily *Las Provincias* pleads that old political animosities be forgotten and that BI be granted recognition he merits as an author.

Bb389 ——, 'VBI', in *Valencia, ciudad abierta*, Val.: Prometeo, 1971, pp. 253-6.
Reflects on achievements, patriotism of Valencia's native son.

Bb390 Onís, Federico de, ed. *La batalla del Marne*, New York: D.C. Heath, 1920, pp. iii-x.
Onís provides preface and introductory biographical sketch for text version of episode from BI's *Los cuatro jinetes del Apocalipsis*.

Bb391 ——, 'El triunfo de BI', *El Sol*, M (13.3.19).
Reports on fabulous success of *Los cuatro jinetes del Apocalipsis* in USA; praises novel; reasons for its popularity.

Bb392 Pacheco, José Emilio, 'VBI', *Revista Universidad de México*, XXI,5 (1966-7), 27-8.
Except for several suggestive interpretations of BI's views on Mexico, Pacheco's comments are unoriginal and marred by factual error.

Bb393 Pagano, José León, 'VBI', in *Al través de la España literaria*, vol. II, B: Maucci, 1904, pp. 163-79.
Interview with BI, Valle-Inclán and R. Soriano. BI's views on contemporary Spanish literature; admits debt to D'Annunzio.

Bb394 Palacio Valdés, Armando, 'BI', *Informaciones* (28.1.28).
His friendship with BI; BI's kindness, loneliness in final years.

Bb395 Palmarocchi, Roberto, 'VBI', *Rassegna Nazionale*, Roma, 3rd series, I (1928), 81-5.
Praises rustic, lyric quality of BI's early novels; easy fame diminished quality of later works.

Bb396 Pamplona, Clemente, 'BI y Portugal', *La Estafeta Literaria*, 364 (1967), 38.
Details on Ptg. translations of BI's works; his 1909 visit to Portugal.

Bb397 París, Luis, '*La catedral*, novela de VBI', *EP* (24.11.03).
How BI conceived and wrote this novel.

Bb398 Pattison, Walter T., in *El naturalismo español*, M: Gredos, 1969, pp. 29; 53; 168-9; 175.
Observations on *costumbrismo* and naturalism in certain Valencian works.

Bb399 Payró Carrió, F., '*Cañas y barro* por VBI', *El Liberal* (14.3.03).
Discusses novel's naturalism, characterization, pathos, artistry.

Bb400 Peers, E. Allison, 'The Real BI', in *St John of the Cross and Other Lectures and Addresses*, London: Faber and Faber, 1946, pp. 169-79. Reprinted from *Contemporary Review*, CXXXIII (1928), 599-604.
First twenty years are basis for solid literary reputation; BI's subsequent works deserve oblivion.

Bb401 Pemán, José María, 'BI en América', *Mundo Hispánico*, XX,228 (1967), 10.
On the Levantine nature of BI's art; comments on his B.A. lecture tour.

Bb402 Pequeño Belcebú, el [pseud.], 'Croniquilla literaria: a un parranda', *EP* (6.5.08).
Answers criticism of an author who, using pseudonym *un parranda*,

attacked *Sangre y arena* in *La Voz*.

Bb403 Pérez, Darío, 'La vuelta al mundo de un novelista', *El Heraldo de Aragón*, Zaragoza (19.4.24).
How BI plans to write account of his world tour.

Bb404 Pérez de Ayala, Ramón, in Ba27, pp. 83-4.
Expresses esteem for BI. Praises force and traditionalism of his style.

Bb405 —, 'El estilo de tercera clase', in *Pequeños ensayos*, M: Biblioteca Nueva, 1963, pp. 176-7.
BI's 'estilo diluído y profuso' explains why he has attracted so many undemanding (third-rate) readers.

Bb406 —, in 'Muerto BI, ¿quién es, a juicio de usted, el primer novelista español?', *Nuevo Mundo*, 1783 (23.3.28).
In answering survey question of F. Verdugo, RPA neither confirms nor denies assumption in the question. He states that only time will tell which novelist is the greatest.

Bb407 —, 'El Sr BI, de vuelta de los EEUU', in *Pequeños ensayos*, M: Biblioteca Nueva, 1963, pp. 177-9.
Hostile article; incorporates comments from R.C. Benchley, Bb68.

Bb408 —, 'Un libro acerca de BI', in *Pequeños ensayos*, M: Biblioteca Nueva, 1963, pp. 173-5.
Skillfully refutes J. Casares's opinions about *Los cuatro jinetes del Apocalipsis* (Bb117) by demonstrating 'razón de fondo' for novel's popularity.

Bb409 Pérez de la Dehesa, Rafael, 'La Editorial Sempere en Hispanoamérica y España', *Revista Iberoamericana*, XXXV (1969), 551-5.
Lists number of copies in Spanish translation of works of 'advanced thinkers' that were published and sold by BI's Ed. Sempere.

Bb410 —, 'Editoriales e ingresos literarios a principios de siglo', *Revista de Occidente*, 71 (1969), 217-28.
Compares earnings of realist and Generation of 1898 authors, with several references to BI.

Bb411 —, 'Zola y la literatura española finisecular', *Hispanic Review*, XXXIX,1 (1971), 49-60.
The nature of Zola's influence on BI; the latter's efforts to promote Zola's works in Spain.

Bb412 Pérez Ferrero, Miguel, 'Dix ans après . . . les trois vies de BI',

Les Nouvelles Littéraires, Paris (26.2.38).
Outlines the most characteristic stages of BI's life.

Bb413 Pérez Restrepo, Arturo, 'Medio siglo de novela española',
Revista Shell, Caracas (12.19.54), 14-21.
Survey includes similarities and differences between BI and Zola.

Bb414 Pérez Solernóu, E., '*El intruso*', *EP* (8.7.04).
Contrasts Galdós's and BI's methods of literary composition.

Bb415 Peseux, Richard H., 'Comptes rendus', *Revue Hispanique*,
IX (1902), 555-9.
Reviews *La barraca* and its French tr. *Terres maudites.*

Bb416 ——, '*La maja desnuda*', *Revue Hispanique*, XV (1906), 856-8.
Negative review of novel.

Bb417 ——, 'VBI, *Sangre y arena*', *Revue Hispanique*, XVIII (1908),
290-4.
Appreciative review of novel's artistry.

Bb418 Petriconi, H., in *Die spanische Literatur der Gegenwart (seit
1870)*, Wiesbaden: Dioskuren Verlag, 1926, pp. 106-8.
Discusses BI's naturalism, borrowings from other writers, and anti-
German novels.

Bb419 Phillips, Henry A., 'VBI', *Saturday Review of Literature*,
IV,29 (1928), 596.
Interview: BI and motion pictures; his plans just before he died.

Bb420 Pi y Margall, Francisco, and F. Pi y Arsuaga, in *Historia de
España en el siglo XIX*, vol. VII, B: M. Seguí, 1902, p.816.
Praises BI's talents as a novelist.

Pigmalión [pseud.], see Meliá Bernabeu, J.M.

Bb421 Pistrocchi, Mario, 'Con BI en días de inquietud y de destierro',
EP (18.7.31).
A Republican from Italy recalls BI's anti-fascism, his scorn for Italian
and Spanish dictatorships.

Bb422 Pita Romero, Leandro, 'Un escritor que no declina: BI',
La Capital, Rosario, Arg. (15.11.67). *

Bb423 Pitollet, Camille, 'A propos de BI', *Bulletin Hispanique*, XXX,3
(1928), 235-49.
Pitollet's self-serving notes stress BI's control of his biographer.

Bb424 ——, 'A propos de Tartarin revolutionnaire: L'histoire de la traduction allemande des *4 Cavaliers de l'Apocalypse* de VBI', *Renaissance d'Occident*, XIV,1 (1925), 123-43. *

Bb425 ——, 'BI à Valence', *Mercure Universel*, XII (Nov.-Dec. 1933), 1-18. *

Bb426 ——, 'BI historien: à propos de Robert de Roncy', *Renaissance d'Occident*, XIV,3 (1925), 727-37. *

Bb427 ——, 'BI sujet de thèse doctorale', *Bulletin Hispanique*, XXXIII,2 (1931), 157-62.

Announces first dissertation on BI is nearly completed. Also lists gallicisms and errors in *Los cuatro jinetes del Apocalipsis*.

Bb428 ——, '*La bodega* de VBI', *Bulletin Hispanique*, VII (1905), 307-9.

Judges work to be Zolaesque in conception. Examines form of its social message.

Bb429 ——, 'Ce que pensent les libertaires de la République Blasquiste', *Renaissance d'Occident*, XV,1 (1925), 129-35.

On arrest of BI's son Sigfrido in Spain; BI, Unamuno and newspaper *España con Honra*; Italian anarchists scorn the writer-politician BI.

Bb430 ——, 'Chronique', *Bulletin Hispanique*, XXXIV,4 (1932), 352-4.

A. Greiner's dissertation on BI, Ba40, is an insignificant booklet revealing great ignorance of the subject.

Bb431 ——, 'Los escritores españoles. In memoriam. *Libro-homenaje al inmortal novelista VBI*', *Revue des Langues Romanes*, LXV,19-24 (1928), 360-4.

Thorough review of homage volume to BI (Ba27).

Bb432 ——, 'L'Inde de BI', *Renaissance d'Occident*, XVII,3 (1926), 325-32.

Why vol. III of *La vuelta al mundo de un novelista* is a banal piece of writing based more on second-hand information than on direct observation.

Bb433 ——, 'Juli Just Gimeno: *BI i València*', *Bulletin Hispanique*, XXXI (1929), 373-82.

Review of Just's biography (Ba47) stresses facts revealed about BI and his family that were concealed by BI and earlier biographers.

Bb434 ——, '*El Papa del mar* par BI', *Renaissance d'Occident*, XIX,1

(1926), 69-77; no. 2, 186-94.

Refutes BI's claim that novel is based on careful research and that it employs a new formula for writing of historical novels.

Bb435 ——, 'Les Précurseurs du roman *sicalíptico*. Une opinion inédite de BI sur la littérature *sicalíptica*. *El águila y la serpiente*', *Le Mercure*, XXIX (1934), 27-40. *

Bb436 ——, 'Quelques notes sur E. Gómez Carrillo et BI', *Renaissance d'Occident*, XXV,1 (1928), 108-13; no. 2, 199-204; no. 3, 432-9; XXVI,1, 61-6.

Mainly criticism of EGC's book on Mata Hari with references to press reports of BI's death.

Bb437 ——, '*Sangre y arena* de VBI', *Bulletin Hispanique*, XI,2 (1909), 200-5.

Balanced, detailed review of novel.

Bb438 ——, 'Sur le dernier recueil de contes de BI: *Novelas de la Costa Azul*', *Renaissance d'Occident*, XII,1 (1924), 181-91.

Facts about French translations of several of BI's recent collections of stories; almost no analysis of works themselves.

Bb439 ——, 'Sur la mort de BI', *Renaissance d'Occident*, XXIV (1928), 373-80.

Pitollet composes largely from judgments of others in the French press a portrait of BI which, although uneven, is interesting for the personal impressions, anecdotes, and certain little-known facts it contains.

Bb440 ——, 'VBI, *A los pies de Venus*', *Revue des Langues Romanes*, LXV,19-24 (1928), 351-60.

Sharp critique of novel's composition and style. Also asserts that BI plagiarized historian Carlos Pereyra in writing *En busca del Gran Kan*.

Bb441 ——, 'VBI, *Estudios literarios*, Val., 1934', *Bulletin Hispanique*, XXXVII,2 (1935), 241-4.

Negative appraisal of BI's articles of literary criticism on French authors.

Bb442 Pla, José, 'BI', in *Grandes tipos*, B: Ed. Aedos, 1959, pp. 59-89.

Shrewd analysis of BI's character and personality with many revealing anecdotes.

Bb443 ——, in *Homenots*, 1ª serie, B: Ed. Selecta, 1960, p.84. *

Bb444 Porterfield, Allen W., 'Three Spaniards', *The Bookman*, LVII,

5 (1923), 576-9.
Naive contrast of BI, Benavente, Martínez Sierra with Cervantes, Calderón, Lope de Vega.

Bb445 Portoles, Miguel, 'El regionalismo en Valencia', *Nuevo Mundo*, 357 (7.11.1900).
BI against perspective of Valencia's artistic regionalism.

Bb446 Prieto, Indalecio, 'Flores sobre una tumba', *EP* (15.2.28).
On BI's passion for justice and love for the people.

Bb447 Puig Torralba, Ramón, 'BI, abogado', *EP* (31.1.28).
BI's sole activity as lawyer was the early defense of two Republicans.

Bb448 Pujol, Juan, 'BI, literato sobre todo', *Informaciones* (28.1.28).
BI's universal fame, his simple joy in his success.

Bb449 Ramón y Cajal, Santiago, in Ba27, p.69.
Has read almost all of BI's works; found them informative and esthetically pleasing.

Bb450 Rascoe, Burton, '*The Four Horsemen of the Apocalypse* by VBI', *Chicago Tribune* (19.10.18).
Review: novel's emotional appeal, lack of hyperbole, indictment of the German people, characterization.

Bb451 Reding, Katherine, 'BI and Zola', *Hispania* (USA), VI,6 (1923), 365-71.
Similarities and differences in novelistic technique and style of two novelists. How Zola influenced BI.

Bb452 Rivas, Fabra, 'La obra de BI en España y en la América Latina', *EP* (21.2.15).
BI combats Prussian militarism in newspapers of Spanish-speaking world.

Bb453 Rivas Cherif, Cipriano, 'Carta abierta a *El Pueblo* en memoria de BI', *EP* (16.2.28).
Recalls BI's generosity and kindness.

Bb454 Robin, Marcel, '*Oriente*', *Mercure de France*, LXXVIII,281 (1909), 179-81.
Biting review of BI's new *itinéraire*, its dubious comparisons and over-simplified psychology.

Bb455 Rodríguez Abarrátegui, 'BI, revolucionario', in *VBI*, Val.: Sempere, 1904, pp. 1-3.
Praises BI's efforts for a republic; in 8pp. pamphlet published on occasion of *velada* for BI by Madrid Republican workers.

Bb456 Rogers, Douglass, 'The Descriptive Simile in Galdós and BI:
A Study in Contrasts', *Hispania* (USA), LIII,4 (1970),
864-9.
Revealingly compares the nature and artistic use of similes in *Fortunata y Jacinta* and *La barraca.*

Bb457 Rojas, Ricardo, 'BI y sus novelas', in *Retablo español*, B.A.:
Losada, 1938, pp. 227-30.
Mostly impressions of BI the man.

Bb458 Romera-Navarro, Miguel, '*Los cuatro caballos del Apocalipsis*,
por VBI' (sic), *La Lectura*, III (1918), pp. 175-6.
Cites glowing critical reviews of novel in America. Speculates on reasons for its unique success among many war novels.

Bb459 Royo Villanova, Antonio, 'Sangre aragonesa: Hablando con
BI', *Heraldo de Aragón*, Zaragoza (10.5.21).
BI's love for the land of his parents.

Bb460 Rubio, Rodrigo, 'En el centenario de BI', *La Estafeta
Literaria*, 363 (1967), 36.
On rebirth in 1966 of once famous Ed. Prometeo founded by BI.

Bb461 Sackett, Theodore A., 'Day, A.G., and Knowlton, E.C.,
Blasco Ibáñez', *Hispania* (USA), LVII,4 (1974), 1013.
Review: excessive plot summary and insufficient esthetic consideration of Valencian novels are major faults of this Twayne Series study on BI (Ba24).

Bb462 —— , 'Symbol, Myth and Naturalism in BI's *Cañas y barro*',
paper read at MLA meeting, Chicago, 1971; revised version
to appear in *Homenaje a Ruth Lee Kennedy*, ed. Vern G.
Williamsen.
Analyses symbolic level of meaning in the ambient and characters of *Cañas y barro*, a mythological world where power of nature is absolute.

Bb463 Sacks, Norman P., 'Los chuetas de Mallorca y *Los muertos
mandan*', *Davar*, B.A., 120 (1969), 96-122.
See Ba86 for description of this article.

Ba464 Sainte-Croix, J.L., 'BI', *Mercure de France*, CLIV (15.3.22),
595-612.
Essay intended to present BI and his works 'dans une étude d'ensemble au public français'.

Bb465 —— , *Mare Nostrum* par VBI', *Bulletin Hispanique*, XX,1

(1918), 56.
German outrages moved BI to express feelings about the war.

Bb466 Salaverría, José María, 'La novela del renacimiento', *La Nación*, B.A. (12.6.27).
Review: *A los pies de Venus.*

Bb467 ——, 'Los secretos de la literatura', *La Nación*, B.A. (9.8.22).
Financial success and expatriation have distorted BI's perception of the Spanish character.

Bb468 Salgado Faura, F., '*Cañas y barro* por VBI', *El Liberal* (22.4.03).
Long essay; defines essential traits of novel's main characters.

Bb469 Salinas, Pedro, 'El concepto de generación literaria aplicada a la del 98', in *Literatura española siglo XX*, M: Alianza, 1970, p.32.
Mentions Generation of '98's 'justa injusticia' towards BI.

Bb470 Sánchez, Alberto, 'Curiosa fuente de un pasaje de BI', *Revista Valenciana de Filología*, I,1 (1951), 73-88.
Debt of BI's *En busca del Gran Kan* to F. Maldonado de Guevara's *El primer contacto de blancos y gentes de color en América.*

Bb471 Sánchez, Federico, '*A los pies de Venus*, por VBI', *Hispania* (USA), X,4 (1927), 380-1.
Novel is informative and well written but lacks a sharply delineated protagonist.

Bb472 Sanchis Guarner, M., 'La generació de *Lo rat penat* (1878-1907)', in *Renaixença al país valencià,* Val.: Col·lecció tres i quatre, 1968, pp. 47-68.
BI's admiration for C. Llombart, founder of *Lo Rat Penat*. Cultural and political reasons for BI's subsequent rejection of *Lo Rat Penat* and why he did not write in Valencian.

Bb473 Santibáñez Puga, Fernando [pseud: Santiván, Fernando], 'BI, conferenciante', in *Confesiones de Santiván*, *OC*, vol. II, Santiago: Zig-Zag, 1965, pp. 1671-9.
On hostile reaction of Chilean press to BI's 1910 (sic) lecture tour.

Bb474 Santillán, Ignacio de, 'Santillán, sí', *EP* (12.3.04).
Reiterates his vote for giving BI national honors.

Santiván, F. [pseud.] See Santibáñez Puga, Fernando.

Bb475 Sarrailh, Jean, 'BI', in *Prosateurs espagnols contemporains,*

Paris: Librairie Delagrave, 1930, pp. 93-6.
Perceptive introduction to BI's works; followed by passages from novels, pp. 96-109.

Schraibman, José: see Nuez, Sebastián de la, and Schraibman, José.

Bb475a Sevilla, Alberto, '*Sangre y arena*', in *Gazapos Literarios*, Murcia: Imp. Sucesores de Nogués, 1909, pp. 263-9.
Praises happy combination of BI's descriptive skills and imagination in this taurine novel.

Bb476 Sichel, Walter, '*The Three Knights of the Apocalypse*' (sic), *The Nineteenth Century*, LXXXIII,496 (1918), 1236-48.
Analyses novel's realism and emphasis on German savagery in War. Provides explanation of BI's treatment of War for readers who will soon have an English translation of the novel.

Bb477 Silva Vildósola, Carlos, 'VBI', in *Retratos y recuerdos*, Santiago: Zig-Zag, 1936, pp. 245-60.
Exaggerates BI's affection for Chile, but otherwise provides valuable information about BI's visit there.

Bb478 Siros, Clara Lou, 'VBI: *El adiós de Schubert*, Ed. Cosmópolis', *Books Abroad*, II,2 (1928), 42.
In referring to items published under above title, reviewer seems unaware that they are reprints of one of BI's youthful repudiated works.

Bb479 Smith, Paul, 'BI and Drama', *Hispanófila*, 46 (1972), 35-40.
On BI's only play, *El juez*.

Bb480 ——, 'BI and the Theme of the Jews', *Hispania* (USA), LVI, Special Issue (1973), 282-94.
BI's literary treatment of the Jews; changing attitudes towards them as reflected in his fiction and journalistic writing.

Bb481 ——, 'On BI's *Flor de Mayo*', *Symposium*, XXIV,1 (1970), 55-66.
Flor de Mayo as a model for *Cañas y barro*. Probable literary influences on *Flor de Mayo* itself.

Bb482 ——, 'Seven Unknown Articles by the Future Azorín', *Modern Language Notes*, LXXXV,2 (1970), 250-1.
Introduction to articles treats Azorín's relationship with BI and his collaboration in BI's *El Pueblo*.

Bb483   Sobejano, Gonzalo, 'VBI', in *Nietzsche en España*, M:
Gredos, 1967, pp. 430-8.
BI took from Nietzsche 'argumentos, no actitudes integrales frente a
la vida'. Perceptive exposition of Nietzschean influence in five of BI's
novels.

Bb484   Sociedad Tipográfica de Valencia, 'Al público -
Antecedentes - BI con careta - La huelga de *El Pueblo* -
BI sin careta', *Suplemento al Boletín 54* (25.5.99).
Tries to prove that BI, owner of *EP*, cynically proclaims himself
friend of working class while he exploits his workers and fires those
who dare to complain.

Bb485   —, ' ¡Fuera farsantes! - La vida de *El Pueblo*. Las víctimas
de BI', *Suplemento al Boletín 54* (26.5.99).
Details on strike at *EP*. Refutes BI's defense against accusations that
he exploits his workers.

Bb486   Solano, Armando, 'VBI', *Repertorio Americano*, XVI,7
(1928), 122-3.
Distinguishes the earlier talented writer and revolutionary from the
subsequent 'manufacturer of books'.

Bb487   Soldevilla, F.,'*La horda*, novela por VBI', *EP* (13.7.05).
Praises exactness of BI's presentation of subject matter in *La horda*.

Bb488   Soler Godes, E., 'Dimoni y los otros', *Las Provincias*, Val.
(29.1.67).
Observations on memorable characters in BI's short stories.

Bb488a   Soriano, Rodrigo, 'Blasco en el poder', in *La entrada de
Nozaleda*, M: Cosmópolis, 1904, pp. 217-35.
Satirical fantasy on what life would be like in a city completely con-
trolled by Blasquistas.

Bb489   Souday, Paul,'Les Livres', *Le Temps* (3.4.12).
Analyses five of BI's early novels. Perceptively compares them to
French and Italian works.

Bb490   Starkie, Walter, 'BI, 1867-1928', *Nineteenth Century*, CIII,
1614 (1928), 542-59.
Although impressionistic, this résumé of life and works contains
some perceptive observations on BI.

Bb491   —, 'Some Novelists of Modern Spain', *Nineteenth
Century*, XCVIII,583 (1925), 452-61.
Comments on BI, Galdós, Unamuno, Baroja; occasional comparisons

to English-language novelists.

Bb492 Sternheim, Klaus, 'Von Ibáñez zu Unamuno', *Deutsche Rundschau*, LIII,210 (1927), 76-7.
Compares BI and Gerhart Hauptmann. Observations on BI and other novelists.

Bb493 Suasus, M., 'Mercado de libros: *La bodega*', *La Publicidad* (24.4.05).
On novel's epic dimension, characterization, pictorial art.

Bb494 —, 'Mercado de libros: *El intruso*', *La Publicidad* (3.7.04).
Characterization of S. Morueta and depiction of pilgrimage are novel's strengths. Doctrine and psychological superficiality are its weaknesses.

Bb495 —, 'Mercado de libros: El viaje de BI a América', *La Publicidad* (3.1.05).
Praises BI's forthcoming lecture tour to promote Spanish books in Spanish America.

Bb496 Surió, Luis, 'El temperamento de BI', in *Artistas valencianos*, Val.: Tipografía P. Quiles, 1967, pp. 27-43.
Interpretation of BI's personality based on analysis of his childhood relationship to his parents.

Bb497 Swain, James O., 'The Albufera Thirty Years After', *Hispania* (USA), XVIII,1 (1935), 25-36.
A visit to the Albufera reveals how much passage of time has altered setting of *Cañas y barro*.

Bb498 —, '*Sónnica la cortesana*, and Present-Day Sagunto', *Hispania* (USA), XXI,2 (1938), 75-82.
Recalls visit to Sagunto described in BI's novel.

Bb499 Tailhade, Laurent, 'VBI', *Hispania*, Paris, I,1 (1918), 8-16.
Essay presenting BI as one of the great authors and champions of liberty of his time.

Bb500 Tenreiro, Ramón María, '*Los argonautas* por VBI', *La Lectura*, XIV,3 (1914), 467-9.
Novel represents a continuation rather than an evolution in BI's art.

Bb501 —, '*Los cuatro jinetes del Apocalipsis*, por VBI', *La Lectura*, XVI,2 (1916), 69-71.
This naturalistic epic, with its powerful description of war, recalls Zola's *Le Débâcle*. Madariaga is one of BI's best creations.

Bb502 —, '*Luna Benamor*, por VBI', *La Lectura*, IX,2 (1909),

430-1.
Work lacks structure of a novel. Comments on accompanying pieces.

Bb503 ——, '*Mare Nostrum*, novela por VBI', *La Lectura*, XVIII, 3 (1918), 63-5.
Although depiction of sea is outstanding, plot is too complex and novel's protagonists are lifeless.

Bb504 ——, '*Los muertos mandan*, por VBI', *La Lectura*, IX, 2 (1909), 64-6.
A balanced review treating all aspects of the novel.

Bb505 Ternovski, E., 'BI en las traducciones rusas', *Literatura Soviética*, Moscow, 8 (1967), 170-1. *

Bb506 Thiébaut, Marcel, 'Retorno a BI', *La Nación*, B.A. (30.10.38).
Excellent article. Explains French enthusiasm for BI's works. Also BI's ideas on revolution, the Republic; his enthusiasm for life and for work.

Bb507 ——, 'VBI', *La Revue de Paris*, XXV, 1 (1928), 919-37.
General study; BI as a supporter of noble causes.

Bb508 Tominaga, H., 'El día 23 y el 24 de diciembre de 1923. BI en Japón', *Hispánica*, Tokyo, XII (1967), 26-43; XIII (1968), 26-9. *

Bb509 Toro y Gisbert, Miguel, in *Apuntaciones lexicográficas*, Paris: P. Ollendorff, n.d., pp. 200-15.
Words from *Los muertos mandan* that are candidates for inclusion in Real Academia's dictionary.

Bb510 —— , 'El vocabulario de BI', in *Los nuevos derroteros del idioma*, Paris: R. Roger-F. Chernoviz, 1918, pp. 8-15.
BI is one of 'notables constructores del idioma castellano'; lists words from *La catedral* that should be included in Real Academia's dictionary.

Bb511 Torre, Guillermo de, 'BI, colonizador', in *Vigencia de Rubén Darío y otras páginas*, M: Guadarrama, 1969, pp. 179-82.
On difficulty of classifying BI's works; observations on his Argentine colonizing misadventures.

Bb512 Torrente Ballester, Gonzalo, 'BI', in *Panorama de la literatura española contemporánea*, vol. I, M: Guadarrama, 1961, pp. 129-31.
A sharply hostile sketch of BI that admits almost nothing positive about his works.

Bb513 Tovar, Antonio, 'BI y la historia', *Papeles de Son Armadans*,

XXVIII,84 (1963), 307-11.
Solid review of M. Domínguez Barberá's book on BI, Ba25.

Bb514 Trullenque, Rafael, 'Maestros contemporáneos: BI y Azorín', *EP* (27.3.15).
Disputes Azorín's comments on BI's literary style.

Bb515 Ugarte, Manuel, 'La última novela de BI', *EP* (28.12.04).
Attacks idea of art for art's sake. BI's *El intruso* is the most 'social' novel published in Spain and BI is in the tradition of Zola, Santos Chocano, and the Rubén Darío of 'Canto a Roosevelt'.

Bb516 ——, 'VBI', in *Visiones de España*, Val.: Prometeo, 1925, pp. 101-4.
BI's skills as artist and orator; his universality of spirit.

Bb517 Unamuno, Miguel de, '*La Bogería* de Narciso Oller', *OC*, vol. V, B: Vergara, 1958, p.601.
Compares novel to BI's *La barraca.*

Bb518 ——, 'Con el palo en el bombo', *OC*, vol. X, B: Vergara, 1958, p.430.
Galdós's best novel is superior to best novel of BI, Valera, Pereda.

Bb519 ——, 'De arte pictórica', *OC*, vol. XI, B: Vergara, 1958, pp. 557; 562.
BI's treatment of Unamuno's Bilbao in *El intruso* is false and superficial, but his *La barraca* and *Cañas y barro* are admirable novels, for in them BI captures the Valencian soul.

Bb520 ——, 'En memoria de BI', *EP* (29.10.33).
This long article written in 1928 avoids discussion of BI's works, but praises BI as a great patriot, citizen, etc., and is Unamuno's most fraternal evocation of his shared experience as a pro-Republic exile in France.

Bb521 —— , 'La frontera lingüística', *OC*, vol. I, B: Vergara, 1958, pp. 809-11.
Against the background of other authors' works written in Valencian, Unamuno asserts the *valencianismo* of BI's works written in Spanish.

Bb522 ——, 'El jugo de mi raza', *OC*, vol. X, B: Vergara, 1958, p.954.
Claims that it is ridiculous for *La barraca* to have been translated into Catalan because BI thought and wrote in Spanish.

Bb523 —— , 'Literatura y política', *OC*, vol.XI, B: Vergara, 1958, p.665.
Galdós mistakenly believed that BI's political fame was reason why he

sold more works than did Galdós.

Bb524 ——, 'Lo pasajero', *OC*, vol. XI, B: Vergara, p.636.
Cites BI's example of Italian E. De Amicis as proof that public homage is often paid to politicians but rarely to artists.

Bb525 ——, 'Nuestra impresión de Galdós', *OC*, vol. V, B: Vergara, 1958, p.473.
Rejects Galdós's idea of a realistic portrait of a lifeless society. The passionate, profound life is where Pereda found it for *Sotileza* and BI for *La barraca*, 'en las naturalezas bravías y elementales del pueblo del mar o del campo'.

Bb526 ——, 'Reciprocidad hispanoamericana', *OC*, vol. VI, B: Vergara, 1958, p.918.
Compares Hugo Wast's *Valle Negro* to BI's 'inmortal *La barraca*'.

Bb527 ——, in *OC*, vol. III, B: Vergara, 1958, p.39.
Criticizes attempt to destroy people's belief in an afterlife through BI's tradition of 'europeización (!!!) por esas horrendas bibliotecas de avulgaramiento'. (Reference is to BI's 'Biblioteca Popular', Ed. Sempere.)

Bb528 ——, in *OC*, vol. V, B: Vergara, p.389.
In sentimental Portugal one more easily finds translations of Pérez Escrich than of Galdós, or even of the widely read BI.

Bb529 ——, in *OC*, vol. VIII, B: Vergara, 1958, p.633.
Expresses amusement that American translations purge amorous passage from *Mare Nostrum.*

Bb530 ——, in *OC*, vol. XVI, B: Vergara, 1958, p.667.
A novelist should not read other authors' works although BI asserts 'él apenas lee más que novelas'.

Bb531 Underhill, John Garrett, 'Introduction' to Eng. tr. of *La barraca*, Ae3, pp. 1-7.
Contains perceptive observations on BI's character and literary style.

Bb532 Valentín, Faustino, 'BI', in *VBI*, Val.: Sempere, 1904, pp. 5-6.
Comments on BI's temperament and literary style in 8pp. pamphlet published on occasion of *velada* for BI by Madrid Republican workers.

Bb533 Valera, Juan, in *OC*, vol. III, M: Aguilar, 1958, pp. 559-60.
On BI, Pardo Bazán and the authorship of short story 'La Chucha'.

Bb534 Valle-Inclán, Ramón del, *Informaciones* (28.1.28). *
Never read BI's works except for fragments of *La barraca* in *El Liberal*; doubts that BI has died. Reports of his death are probably a trick to gain attention.

Bb535 Vargas, José E., 'Releyendo a BI en su centenario', *Índice de Artes y Letras*, M, XXII, 217-18 (1967), 69-70.
It is important to break curtain of silence that has surrounded BI's person and works in Spain since 1939.

Bb536 Vargas, Luis de, 'VBI: *La horda*', *La República de las Letras* (1.7.05).
Demonstrates that *La horda* and *La bodega* represent an artistic advance over two previous novels. Asserts that *La horda*'s realism-naturalism relates it to the Valencian novels.

Bb537 Vásquez Cey, Arturo, '*La barraca*, novela mediterránea', *Humanidades*, Univ. de la Plata, XXIV (1934), 281-312. Also reprinted as a pamphlet: B.A.: J. Menéndez, 1935, 34pp.
One of better studies on *La barraca*. Examines novel's epic vein, structure, regionalism, characters.

Bb538 Vayssière, Jean, 'Émile Zola présenté par BI dans *El Pueblo* (1897-1903)', in *Recherches sur le monde hispanique et hispanoaméricain au dix-neuvième siècle*, III, Lille: Univ. de Lille - Éditions Universitaires,1973,pp.259-74.
Concludes that BI admired in Zola the public *engagé* figure more than the artist.

Bb539 Verdugo, Francisco, 'Muerto BI, ¿quién es, a juicio de usted, el primer novelista español?', *Nuevo Mundo*, 1783 (23.3.28).
The following are among many authors who give diverse answers to Verdugo's question: R. López de Haro, Emilio Carrere, Alberto Insúa, José Más, W. Fernández Flórez, Concha Espina, R. Pérez de Ayala: Bb406. Some dispute assertion that BI's popularity made him the first novelist of Spain. Most list Palacio Valdés or Baroja as first among living Spanish novelists.

Bb540 Vézinet, F., '*La maja desnuda*', in *Les Maîtres du roman espagnol contemporain*, Paris: Hachette, 1907, pp. 256-79.
Detailed account of plot construction; analysis of Renovales's character; weakness of final chapter.

Bb541 ——, 'Les Personnages d'Ibáñez', in *Les Maîtres du roman espagnol contemporain*, Paris: Hachette, 1907, pp. 235-55. This is a slightly revised version of article in *Revue Latine* (25.5.06), 303-20.
BI, a vigorous man, infuses his characters with a strong drive for success, hence the predominance of single-minded, strong-willed protagonists. The occasional weak, ineffectual character is used for contrast.

Bb542 Vickers, Peter, 'VBI: literatura e ideología (1880-1905)', in
Siete temas sobre historia contemporánea del país valenciano,
Ciclo de Conferencias de la Facultad de Filosofía y Letras,
ed. José Manuel Cuenca Toribio, Val.: Univ. de Valencia,
1974, pp. 175-203.
On the impossibility of understanding BI's works from an exclusively
literary viewpoint. This interesting essay stresses the socio-political
meaning of BI's works. Among its many original and thought-provoking
interpretations is that of the relative optimism of the Valencian and
the thesis novels.

Bb543 Vidal Corella, Vicente, 'VBI, escritor de Valencia', *Las
Provincias*, Val. (29.1.67).
Mainly observations on BI's childhood, youth, early works.

Bb544 Vilanova, María, in *Un drama del espacio . . . dictado por el
espíritu de Blasco a María Vilanova, del grupo 'Amor y Vida'*,
B: Imprenta Rubí, 1934, 122pp. *
Apparently a work involving some spiritualistic communication with BI.

Bb545 Villaseca, Rafael, 'El valencianismo del maestro', *Blanco y
Negro*, 1917 (12.2.28).
BI's enduring love for Valencia.

Bb546 —, 'Viajes de *ABC*: de paso en Niza', *ABC* (4.9.21).
BI at work during a quiet Riviera summer.

Bb547 Villena, Mestre Juan de [pseud.?], 'La huella de VBI', *Revista
Americana de Buenos Aires*, 74 (1930), 44-7.
BI's role in introducing modern ideas in Spain; the importance of
financial considerations in three periods of his career.

Bb548 Vinaixa, J. Jorge, 'Dice BI', *EP* (14.5.08).
Long interview: BI as a correspondent of Spanish-American newspapers
and as a book publisher.

Bb549 —, 'La novela *Entre naranjos*', *Nuevo Mundo*, 361
(5.12.1900).
Does not consider this a Valencian novel; lauds its treatment of music.

Bb550 Wahl, F., 'BI', *Frankfurter Zeitung* (31.1.28). *

Bb551 Weiss, Suzanne, 'The Generation of '98 and the Hispanic
Society', *Hispania* (USA), LI (1968), 629-34.
Includes list of documents concerning BI held by Hispanic Society of
America.

Bb552 Wells, Warren B., 'VBI', in *Great Spanish Short Stories*,
Boston: Houghton Mifflin, 1932, pp. 119-21.
Introduction to BI's work precedes translation of story 'Dimoni'.

Bb553 Williams, C. Scott, 'VBI', *Los Angeles School Journal*, III, 23
(1920), 8-9.
Details BI's Los Angeles lecture (31.1.20) promoting interest in Hispanic
culture.

Bb554 Williams, Stanley T., in *The Spanish Background of American
Literature*, New Haven: Yale Univ. Press, 1955, vol. I,
pp. 131-2; vol. II, pp. 264-5.
BI's unparalleled popularity in America; W.D. Howells, J. Dos Passos on
BI.

Bb555 Winkler, Paul, 'Last Words with Ibáñez', *The Living Age*, 334
(1928), 399-402. Tr. from *Neue Freie Presse*, Wien
(15.1.28).
Interview: BI's literary plans; his affection for France and America; his
hope for a world language.

Bb556 Zamacois, Eduardo, 'Perfiles psicológicos de un luchador',
Informaciones (28.1.28).
Portrait of BI; his friendship with *torero* Manolo Granero; BI as a writer
of prologues and a friend of young authors.

Bb557 ——, 'Unas líneas ... BI', *EP* (29.10.33).
BI follows naturalism only in *Arroz y tartana*; differences between Zola
and BI.

Bb558 Zárate, Cristóbal, 'VBI', *El Mercurio*, Santiago-Valparaíso
(14.11.09).
BI's attractive presence; interest his visit has created in Chile.

Bb559 Zavala, Iris, in *Fin de siglo: modernismo, 98 y bohemia*, M:
Cuadernos para el Diálogo, 1974, p.14.
On BI's articles in the periodical *Don Quijote*.

Zeda [pseud.] see Fernández Villegas, Francisco.

Bb560 Zozaya, Antonio, 'Crónica: *La maja desnuda*', *EP* (20.6.06).
Novel constitutes protest against false education of women.

Bb561 Anon, 'La Academia de la Novela', *ABC* (10.1.24).
BI will establish academy with 20,000 peseta annual prize for best novel.

Bb562 ——, *'Argentina y sus grandezas*: juicios sobre *La Nación'*,

B.A. (9.8.10).
Examines book, especially its references to *La Nación.*

Bb563 ——, 'Los argentinos ante el criterio europeo', *La Prensa*, B.A. (14.12.09).
Contrasts BI's sympathy for and understanding of Argentina with more typical European ignorance and condescension.

Bb564 ——, 'The Author of *The Four Horsemen*', *Outlook*, XLVIII,6 (1928), 216-17.
Notes on BI's fame and talent.

Bb565 ——, 'The Author of *The Four Horsemen* a Visitor', *Los Angeles Daily Times* (23.1.20).
Covers all of BI's activities planned for southern California visit.

Bb566 ——, 'BI', *New York Times*, sect. III (2.11.19).
Editorial praising and welcoming BI to America; hopes he will write a novel on America's national sport, baseball.

Bb567 ——, 'BI, A Historian Goes Far Astray', *New York Times* (6.11.19).
Refutes BI's claim that Spain's anemia results from giving her best blood and talent for development of the New World.

Bb568 ——, 'BI Attacks Mexican Militarism', *Current Opinion*, LXIX,1 (1920), 88-90.
Synthesis and analysis of *New York Times* articles against Mexican militarism.

Bb569 —— , 'BI en América', *EP* (11.1.07).
On BI's being named literary correspondent of *La Nación*, B.A.

Bb570 ——, 'BI en la cárcel', *Nuevo Mundo* (9.11.98).
Incarceration of deputy BI for article not submitted to military censor.

Bb571 ——, 'BI en el extranjero', *EP* (19.1.06).
On BI's growing fame and translations of his works.

Bb572 ——, 'BI en la Sorbona', *EP* (22.2.15).
BI's participation in celebration honoring Latin fraternalism.

Bb573 ——, 'BI Ill', *New York Times* (30.1.20).
Nature of BI's illness and physician's report.

Bb574 ——, 'BI, político', *Informaciones* (28.1.28).
Different periods of BI's political activity.

Bb575 ——, 'BI se halla gravísimo a consecuencia de una bronco-

neumonía', *El Sol* (28.1.28).
Series of reports from many cities dealing with medical reports, rumors, family preparations, etc., in connection with BI's deteriorating condition.

Bb576 ——, 'BI, Tarkington, Anthony Hope', *New York Times Review of Books* (17.8.19).
Appreciative review of *Mare Nostrum*; comparison with *The Four Horsemen.*

Bb577 ——, 'BI: The Stormy Petrel of Spain', *The Literary Digest*, XCVI,8 (1928), 41-2; 44-5.
Interesting anecdotes; includes actor Otis Skinner's experiences with BI.

Bb578 ——, 'BI y *Cuba Contemporánea*', *Cuba Contemporánea*, XX, 78 (1919), 318-19.
BI promises to contribute to journal; his plans for Cuban visit.

Bb579 ——, 'Causa contra BI', *El Liberal* (16.12.24).
Military government's charges against BI for publication of *Una nación secuestrada.*

Bb580 ——, 'Colonización en Corrientes', *La Prensa*, B.A. (15.11.10).
Specific details of province's concession of land to BI, criticism it arouses and BI's response.

Bb581 ——, 'Cómo escribía BI', *EP* (11.2.28).
Rough draft of essay on Zola in BI's hand and expanded typed version of the same piece. Comments on how he wrote.

Bb582 ——, 'Correspondencias', *El Socialista*, M (18.7.08).
Blames BI for destroying Valencia's Socialist party by legislating as his own the pro-labor measures originally proposed by Socialists.

Bb583 ——, 'Corrientes', *La Prensa*, B.A. (18.7.11).
Account of Valencian farmers' strike against BI's Nueva Valencia colony.

Bb584 ——, 'Corrientes: La colonización BI', *La Prensa*, B.A. (10.11.10).
BI's plans for developing Rincón Lagraña land concession.

Bb585 ——, 'Corrientes: Los pleitos oficiales', *La Prensa*, B.A. (23.6.11).
Suit before Supreme Court to invalidate province's expropriation of lands for BI's colony.

Bb586 ——, 'Las dedicatorias de Valle-Inclán son auténticas', *EP*

(18.2.28).
Reproduces two dedications alongside verified dedications and calligraphy expert's opinion to prove Valle-Inclán dedicated works to BI. See also Bb617, 634.

Bb587 ——, 'Día a día: el peligro de BI', *El Mercurio*, Santiago-Valparaíso (18.11.09).
Assuages fears that the eloquent BI is a threat to Church and traditions.

Bb588 ——, 'Don VBI', *El Mercurio*, Santiago-Valparaíso (15.11.09).
Introduction to BI's life and career for Chilean readers.

Bb589 ——, 'Don VBI: su llegada - programa de la recepción', *La Nación*, B.A. (6.6.09).
Detailed account of grandiose reception planned for BI.

Bb590 ——, 'En honor de BI', *EP* (17.12.06).
Entire page dedicated to diverse activities of Valencian homage to BI.

Bb591 —— , '¿Escribe el espíritu de BI?', *La Gaceta Literaria* (1.12.28).
Ironic commentaries on Ed. Cosmópolis's sudden publication of BI's forgotten and repudiated youthful writings.

Bb592 —— , 'The Feminine Mystery', *New York Times* (3.3.20).
On BI's over-simplified analysis of the emancipated American woman.

Bb593 —— , 'El futuro libro del Sr BI', *La Prensa*, B.A. (28.7.09).
Extensive account of BI's travels in Argentina and his plans to write *Argentina y sus grandezas.*

Bb594 ——, 'George Washington University Honors Ibáñez', *Bulletin of Pan American Union*, L,5 (1920), 525-31.
Conferring of honorary Doctorate of Letters. Text of Univ. President's address and English tr. of BI's address.

Bb595 ——, 'Los grandes amores de BI', *EP* (29.10.33).
On BI's love for music, Victor Hugo, the Republic, Valencia.

Bb596 ——, 'Gritos de la alcantarilla', *EP* (30.1.28).
Personal attack on Baroja and Valle-Inclán for comments on BI and their dislike of Mediterranean Spaniards.

Bb597 ——, 'Hablando con BI', *Diario Universal* (26.3.07).
On rumors as to why BI retired from Cortes and his future political plans.

Bb598 ——, 'Hablando con BI', *Día Gráfico* (10.6.15).
BI on the European War. Spain's neutrality, etc.

Bb599 ——, 'Homenaje nacional a BI', *El Sol* (31.10.33).
Entire page dedicated to return of BI's mortal remains to Valencia and ceremonies honoring him. Includes address by President of Spanish Republic.

Bb600 ——, 'Honras a VBI', *La Gaceta Literaria* (1.2.28).
Why, although BI's works were of little interest to editors of *La Gaceta Literaria*, BI himself was of great interest to them and the entire Hispanic world.

Bb601 ——, 'Hosts to BI', *New York Times* (22.2.20).
On formal dinner given by former American Minister to Spain.

Bb602 ——, 'Ibáñez Answers Attacks', *New York Times* (13.11.19).
BI answers those who attacked his defense of Spain's role in history of Mexico. Claims antagonists are pro-German sympathizers.

Bb603 ——, 'Ibáñez As a Revolutionist', *The Literary Digest*, LXXXIII,11 (1924), 31.
Concludes that BI's book, intended to help bring down Spain's monarchy, is too dull to incite anyone to revolution.

Bb604 ——, 'Ibáñez Here to Get Copy for Novels', *New York Times* (28.10.19).
First report and interview with BI in America. Plans to gather material for several books on America.

Bb605 ——, 'Ibáñez Mexican Union Club's Guest', *New York Times* (12.11.19).
BI's interest in Mexico. Trip planned to collect material on Mexico for BI's next book.

Bb606 ——, 'Ibáñez Starts Poe Fund', *New York Times* (18.11.19).
Visits Edgar Allan Poe's cottage and gives $100 towards Poe memorial.

Bb607 ——, 'Ibáñez Sued for $6,982', *New York Times* (24.12.19).
Buenos Aires export firm attaches BI's book and lecture royalties.

Bb608 ——, 'Ibáñez to Mobilize Us', *The Literary Digest*, LXIII,8 (1919).
Perceptive observation on *The Four Horsemen of the Apocalypse*. BI's interview for *New York Evening Post* on President Wilson, USA and Spanish America.

Bb609 ——, '*El intruso*: nuevo triunfo de BI', *EP* (1.12.06).
Reproduces opinions from Madrid press on first presentation of play adapted from BI's novel.

Bb610 ——, 'Llegada de BI', *La Prensa*, B.A. (7.6.09).
Long account of BI's arrival in Buenos Aires, ceremonies, transfer to hotel, activities in the afternoon.

Bb611 ——, 'La manifestación republicana', *Nuevo Mundo*, 391 (3.7.01).
Meeting in Retiro against Jubileo Santo; BI, A. Lerroux, R. Soriano participate.

Bb612 ——, *'The Mob'*, *Saturday Review of Literature*, IV,14 (1927), 262.
Review of *La horda*.

Bb613 ——, 'La muerte de BI', *La Esfera* (4.2.28), 21-8.
Informative account with fifteen photographs and short passages from several of BI's works.

Bb614 ——, 'La muerte de BI', *El Sol* (29.1.28).
Useful summary of impressions and notices of BI's death as reported in Spanish and foreign press.

Bb615 ——, 'Notas biográficas', *EP* (29.1.28).
BI's death brings forth review of his life and accomplishments.

Bb616 —— , *'Novelas de la Costa Azul'*, *La Nación* (19.10.24).
Analysis of each story in collection.

Bb617 ——, 'Nuevo autógrafo irrecusable', *EP* (12.2.28).
More on authenticity of Valle-Inclán's dedication of books to BI. See also Bb586, 634.

Bb618 ——, 'Otra gran obra de BI', *Nuevo Mundo*, 1543 (17.8.23).
On BI's *La reina Calafia*.

Bb619 ——, 'Perfiles del día: *La horda*', *El Imparcial* (23.6.05).
Summary of just-published novel and explanation of how BI documented this work.

Bb620 ——, 'Poe and BI', *New York Times* (23.11.19).
BI's admiration for Poe. Differences between the two authors.

Bb621 ——, 'Una prohibición incalificable', *EP* (18.6.15).
Banquet and homage to BI have been suspended in Valencia by governor on pretext they may endanger Spain's neutrality.

Bb622 ——, 'The Revealer of Spain', *The Literary Digest*, LX,7 (1919), 30-1.
Prior to BI's war novel, American public was indifferent to all modern Spanish literature. Short introduction to BI and his works.

Bb623 ——, 'La revolución de Valencia', *EP* (12.3.06).
Long account of BI's accomplishments in modernizing city of Valencia.

Bb624 ——, 'La salud de BI', *EP* (28.1.28).
Many details about BI's medical record, rapidly failing health, etc.

Bb625 ——, '*Sangre y arena*', *ABC* (8.5.08).
Details on latest novel; prediction of great success.

Bb626 ——, 'Se sella el féretro después de depositar en él flores y tierra de Valencia', *El Sol* (31.1.28).
Details on preparation for funeral in France, manifestation of sympathy throughout the world, etc.

Bb627 ——, 'Semana burguesa', *El Socialista*, M (7.2.02).
Attacks BI's Republican coalition in Valencia for its negative attitude towards the working class.

Bb628 ——, 'El 60º aniversario de una colonia fundada por VBI', *La Prensa*, B.A. (22.4.71).
How BI's colony in Corrientes has become a thriving center of rice production for the entire Republic.

Bb629 ——, 'El solemne trasllat de les despulles de BI', *La Publicitat* (31.10.33).
Succinct account of homage to BI in Valencia; Catalan delegation's participation in ceremonies.

Bb630 ——, 'Spain Sees Herself', *The Nation*, CVIII, 2811 (1919), 876.
On *Sangre y arena* and Baroja's *César o nada* in English translation.

Bb631 ——, 'Spain through the Pen of BI', *The Touchstone*, VI, 4 (1920), 214-15.
BI's life, works, ideals summarized for readers of this art magazine.

Bb632 ——, 'Two Novels from the Spanish', *The Nation*, CVI, 2749 (1918), 265.
Detailed introductions to English translations of BI's *La barraca* and Baroja's *La feria de los discretos.*

Bb633 ——, '2000 at Ibáñez Reception', *New York Times* (15.11.19).
On BI's speaking in aid of Actors Fund campaign; reception for BI caused traffic jams at Lyceum Theatre.

Bb634 ——, 'Valle-Inclán desmentido', *EP* (7.2.28).
Publishes copy of Valle-Inclán's dedication of *Sonata de otoño* to BI. See also Bb586, 617.

Bb635 ——, 'El viaje del señor BI', *El Día Gráfico* (20.6.15).
Refutes claims of conservative press that purpose of BI's return visit to Spain is to campaign against Spanish neutrality and for allies.

Bb636 ——, *VBI. Descriptor de la tierra valenciana 1867-1928*, Val.: Tipografía P. Quiles, 1961, 8pp.
Article published in pamphlet form on BI's style, Valencian works, etc.

Bb637 ——, 'VBI ha fallecido en Mentón', *La Nación*, B.A. (29.1.28).
Long review of life and works.

Bb638 ——, 'VBI, nuevo corresponsal de *La Nación*', *La Nación*, B.A. (13.12.06).
Introduces BI to readers; announces his collaboration.

Bb639 ——, 'VBI: su regreso del sur', *El Mercurio*, Santiago-Valparaíso (24.11.09).
Account of BI's visit to southern provinces and his scheduled activities in Santiago.

Bb640 ——, 'When Ibáñez Jumped on His Hat and Other Literary Troubles', *The Literary Digest*, LXXIX,1 (1923), 50-5.
James D. Pond, proprietor of lecture bureau, tells of BI's very bad temper; BI had the most comprehensive selection of swear words of any lecturer he ever dealt with.

Bb641 ——, 'The Yankees and Their Ways As Observed by VBI', *The Literary Digest*, LXVII,6 (1920), 57-8.
Lists BI's most notable and perceptive observations on Americans and the American character.

ADDENDA

Bb642 Bravo-Villasante, Carmen, in *Vida y obra de Emilia Pardo Bazán*, M: Revista de Occidente, 1962, pp. 227-9.
BI's early infatuation with and subsequent scorn for EPB. Scandalous stories he spread about her.

Bb643 Lavaud, J.-M, 'Valle-Inclán et la mort de BI', *Bulletin Hispanique*, LXXVI, 3-4 (1974), 376-90.
Examines Valle-Inclán's and Baroja's controversial comments about BI after latter's death and the response in Spanish newspapers by BI's defenders. Concludes that Valle-Inclán lied when he denied having read works by BI.

Bb644 Ramos, Vicente, 'BI, amigo de Rafael Altamira', *La Estafeta Literaria*, 384 (2.12.67), 15-16.
Traces friendship of the two 'levantinos'; similarities and differences in their lives. Includes six very short letters from BI to Altamira.

Bb645 Vayssière, Jean, '*La barraca* devient *Terres maudites*', *Bulletin Hispanique*, LXXVI, 3-4 (1974), 335-52.
Carefully establishes circumstances surrounding G. Hérelle's translation of *La barraca* and importance of that particular translation for BI's literary fame.

INDEX OF BI's WORKS (SECTION B ONLY)

A los pies de Venus, Ba19; Bb27, 69, 440, 466, 471

El adiós de Schubert, Bb478

El águila y la serpiente, Bb223, 225, 435

La araña negra, Bb155, 199

Argentina y sus grandezas, Bb66, 236, 562, 593

Los argonautas, Ba61; Bb500

Arroz y tartana, Bb17, 251, 557

La barraca, Ba14, 60; Bb39, 130, 132, 153, 159, 195, 295, 304, 326, 415, 456, 517, 519, 522, 526, 531, 534, 537, 632, 645

La bodega, Ba61; Bb43, 80, 143, 187, 194, 208, 214, 428, 493, 536

Caerse del cielo, Bb116, 289

Cañas y barro, Ba52; Bb38, 39, 64, 73, 175, 196, 238, 363, 371, 380, 383, 399, 462, 468, 481, 497, 519

La catedral, Ba26, 61; Bb106, 107, 145, 160, 240, 271, 272, 273, 297, 300, 301, 343, 369, 372, 397, 510

'Compasión', Bb99

'La condenada', Bb306

Los cuatro jinetes del Apocalipsis, Ba13; Bb18, 53, 117, 213, 346, 390, 391, 408, 424, 427, 450, 458, 476, 501, 564, 565, 576, 608

Cuentos valencianos, Ba23, 92; Bb20, 198, 488

En busca del Gran Kan, Bb47, 67, 137, 328, 470

Los enemigos de la mujer, Bb202

Entre naranjos, Ba72, 97; Bb174, 549

Los fanáticos, Bb199

El fantasma de las alas de oro, Bb125

Flor de Mayo, Ba13, 39; Bb17, 229, 376, 481

'El golpe doble', Bb268

Guillem Sorolla, Bb10

Historia de la guerra europea de 1914, Bb213

Historia de la revolución española, Bb80

La horda, Bb32, 58, 59, 80, 127, 150, 163, 210, 241, 254, 281, 339, 341, 373, 382, 487, 536, 612, 619

'Impunidad', Bb37

El intruso, Ba13, 61; Bb144, 160, 311, 331, 374, 381, 414, 494, 515, 519, 609

El juez, Bb10, 479

La juventud del mundo, Bb223

Luna Benamor, Bb108, 242, 502

La maja desnuda, Ba26; Bb50, 211, 243, 344, 375, 416, 540, 560

Mare Nostrum, Bb164, 310, 319, 465, 503, 529, 576

'¡Mátala!', Bb308

El militarismo mejicano, Ba76, 83, 84; Bb171, 568

Los muertos mandan, Ba86; Bb245, 315, 463, 504, 509

Narracions valencianes, Bb147

Novelas de amor y de muerte, Bb28, 139.

Novelas de la Costa Azul, Bb336, 438, 616.

Novelas de la guerra, Ba21; Bb115, 158, 234, 275

Novelas de tesis, Ba21, 40, 67, 91, 103; Bb19, 101, 157

Novelas valencianas, Ba9, 10, 12, 21, 25, 26, 30, 38, 40, 43, 44, 53, 63, 89, 91, 92, 103; Bb14, 198, 254, 266, 351, 395

Oriente, Ba65; Bb247, 318, 454

El Papa del mar, Ba19, 37; Bb23, 71, 94, 335, 434

El préstamo de la difunta, Bb215

La reina Calafia, Bb239, 292, 337, 618

Roméu el guerrillero, Bb97

Sangre y arena, Ba66, 71, 80; Bb1, 105, 106, 154, 169, 186, 193, 248, 249, 266, 271, 354, 370, 384, 402, 417, 437, 475a, 625, 630

Sónnica la cortesana, Ba26, 41; Bb97, 359, 498

La tierra de todos, Bb118
'El último león', Bb77
'Un funcionario', Bb306
'Un lobo de mar', Bb48
'Una nación secuestrada', Ba16; Bb89, 579, 603

'Las vírgenes locas', Ba27
¡Viva la República!, Bb199
La voluntad de vivir, Bb223
La vuelta al mundo de un novelista, Bb26, 342, 403, 432

INDEX OF OTHER WRITERS

Abreu, Héctor, Ba71; Bb248

Alarcón, Pedro Antonio de, Ba63

Alas, Leopoldo [Clarín], Ba60; Bb263, 321

Altamira, Rafael, Bb644

Asturias, Miguel Ángel, Bb146

Azorín [pseud.]: see Martínez Ruiz, José

Balzac, Honoré de, Bb313

Baroja, Pío, Ba5, 57, 67; Bb163, 210, 281, 349, 491, 539, 596, 630, 632, 643

Benavente, Jacinto, Bb444

Beyle, Henri [pseud: Stendhal], Ba96

Boccaccio, G., Ba72

Boix, V., Bb317

Calderón de la Barca, Pedro, Bb444

Cervantes, Miguel de, Bb444

Chocano, José Santos, Bb515

Clarín [pseud.]: see Alas, Leopoldo

Costa, Joaquín, Bb345

D'Annunzio, G., Bb1

Darío, Rubén, Bb515

Daudet, Alphonse, Bb79

De Amicis, Edmondo, Bb524

Dos Passos, John, Bb554

Fernández y González, Manuel, Bb267

Flaubert, Gustave, Ba26, 41, 96; Bb359

France, Anatole [pseud.]: see Thibault, Jacques-Anatole-François

Gómez Carrillo, Enrique, Ba73; Bb436

Goncourt, Edmond and Jules, Ba26

Hauptmann, Gerhart, Bb492

Howells, William Dean, Bb367, 554

Hugo, Victor, Bb140, 343, 595

Huysmans, J.K., Ba26; Bb297, 343

Linares Rivas, Manuel, Bb90

Llombart, C., Bb472

Louÿs, Pierre, Bb359

Maldonado de Guevara, F., Bb470

Martínez Ruiz, José [pseud: Azorín], Bb104, 206, 323, 482, 514

Martínez Sierra, Gregorio, Bb444

Maupassant, Guy de, Ba72

Meredith, George, Bb297

Oller, Narciso, Bb517

Palacio Valdés, Armando, Bb110, 539

Pardo Bazán, Emilia, Ba60, 63; Bb156, 256, 533, 642

Pereda, José María de, Bb263, 518, 525

Pérez de Ayala, Ramón, Ba67

Pérez Escrich, Enrique, Bb528

Pérez Galdós, Benito, Ba5, 63, 70; Bb110, 284, 381, 387, 414, 456, 491, 518, 523, 525, 528

Pizcueta, F., Bb317

Poe, Edgar Allan, Bb606, 620

Rodenbach, G., Ba26

Soriano, Rodrigo, Ba73, 101; Bb43, 86, 135, 393, 611

Stendhal [pseud.]: see Beyle, Henri

Thibault, Jacques-Anatole-François [pseud: Anatole France], Bb95, 131

Tolstoy, Leo, Bb238

Unamuno, Miguel de, Ba5, 28, 42; Bb54, 146, 314, 429, 491, 492

Valera, Juan, Bb518

Valle-Inclán, Ramón del, Ba5, 57; Bb133, 259, 393, 586, 596, 617, 634, 643

Vega, Lope de, Bb444

Wast, Hugo, Bb526

Zola, Émile, Ba5, 40; Bb79, 205, 251, 313, 411, 413, 428, 451, 501, 515, 538, 557, 581